THE SANTAL INSURRECTION OF 1855-57

THE SANTAL INSURRECTION
OF 1855-57

BY

KALIKINKAR DATTA, M.A., PH.D. (CAL.)

Premchand Roychand Scholar, Mouat Medallist, Griffith Prizeman, Assistant Professor of History, Patna College, Author of Studies in the History of the Bengal Subah, 1740-70 AD, Education and social Amelioration of women in Pre Mutiny India, 'Alivardi and His Times and Joint Author of 'Text Book of Modern Indian History'.

GYAN

ISBN: 978-81-212-1386-8(HB)

First Published in 1940
Indian Reprint in 2017

Published by

Gyan Publishing House
5, Ansari Road
Daryaganj, New Delhi-110002
Phone: 9811692060
E-mail: books@gyanbooks.com

Cataloging in Publication Data—DK
Courtesy: D.K. Agencies (P) Ltd. <docinfo@dkagencies.com>

Datta, Kalikinkar, 1905-1982, **author.**
The Santal insurrection of 1855-57 / by Kalikinkar Datta.
pages cm
Reprint. Originally published: Calcutta : University of Calcutta, 1940.
Includes index.
ISBN 9788121213868 (HB)

1. Santal Rebellion, 1855-1856. I. Title.

DS485.B49D3 2017 DDC 954.140049595 23

DEDICATED

TO

His Excellency SIR MAURICE GARNIER HALLETT,

K.C.S.I., C.I.E., I.C.S.,

Governor of the United Provinces,

who as commissioner of the Bhagalpur division

and subsequently as governor of Bihar

took a keen interest in the antiquities of the Santal Para-
gaṅas and whose government in Bihar was kind enough to
permit me to utilise its unpublished records
relating to this thesis

CONTENTS

PREFACE

The Santal Insurrection of 1855-57 is an important episode in the annals of Bengal and Bihar during the mid-nineteenth century, which forms, in many ways, a transitional period in the history of India as a whole. It has been so long referred to, rather briefly, by writers like Marshman,[1] Wheeler,[2] Hunter,[3] Lee-Warner,[4] Buckland,[5] Bradley-Birt,[6] L. S. S. O'Malley,[7] and Sir H. Verney Lovett.[8] Recently, certain important original records have been discovered by me and utilised for a detailed and critical study of the subject in this thesis. I have often quoted extracts from the unpublished records, with a view to bringing these to light as far as possible.

These records may be noted under six heads :—

(1) *Contemporary documents in English preserved in the record-room of the Commissioner of the Bhagalpur Division.* These documents consist of

(a) Letters from the Commissioner of Bhagalpur.
(b) Letters to the Commissioner of Bhagalpur.
(c) Grants of rewards, etc., to those who helped the Government in suppressing the insurrection.

(2) *Contemporary documents in English, Bengali, Hindi and Persian, preserved in the record-room of the Deputy Commissioner of the Santal Paraganas, Dumka.* These include despatches, records of cases, etc.

1 *History of India*, Part II, Chapter XL, p. 720.
2 *A Short History of India*, p. 124.
3 *Our Indian Empire*, 3rd Edition, pp. 97-98. *Annals of Rural Bengal*, pp. 230-55
4 *Life of Lord Dalhousie*, Vol. II, pp. 60-65.
5 *Bengal under the Lieutenant-Governors*, Vol. I, pp. 11-16.
6 *Story of an Indian Upland*, Chapter VII
7 *History of Bengal, Bihar and Orissa.* Santal Paraganas District Gazetteer.
8 *Cambridge History of India*, Vol. VI, p. 35.

(3) *'History of the Santal Hool of 1855' by the late Babu Digambar Chakraverty of Pakur in the district of Santal Paraganas, written at the beginning of the twentieth century.* The author was six years old when the Santal insurrection broke out, and he gathered the materials for his work from those who had personal experience of it.

(4) *Manuscript No. 2096 preserved in the Ratan Library, Suri, Birbhum.* It is a contemporary Bengali ballad describing the activities of the Santal insurgents towards Birbhum. From its concluding lines we know that it was composed in the year 1262 B.S. (1855 A.D.), the very year of the outbreak of the insurrection, by Rai Krishnadas, an inhabitant of Kulkuri, a village in the Birbhum district.

(5) *A contemporary Bengali manuscript in prose, being the autobiography of a gentleman, belonging to a Maratha family settled at Karum,* a village in the Deoghur subdivision of the district of Santal Paraganas. We know from internal evidence in the text that the writer himself took some part in the suppression of the insurrection. He gives a detailed description of the ravages, committed by the Santal insurgents, round about and also within the area of his village.

(6) *A Bengali ballad giving many important details about the insurrection.* It was composed during the end of the 19th century by the late Babu Dhana Krishna Ruj, Bazar Chowdhury of Panchkethia in the Rajmahal subdivision of the district of Santal Paraganas.

(7) Contemporary English papers and journals like 'The Friend of India' and 'The Calcutta Review,' etc.

I submitted a paper on 'Original Records about the Santal Insurrection' at the Seventh All-India Oriental Conference at Baroda and got it published in 'Bengal: Past and Present,' Vol. XLVIII, Part I. The Editor of 'Bengal: Past and Present,' also very kindly published certain sections of this thesis in his journal in 1934 and 1936, for which I thank him sincerely.

I take this opportunity of expressing my gratitude and thankfulness to those who have helped me in the preparation of this work. I am greatly indebted to the Government of Bihar, to the Commissioner of the Bhagalpur Division, and to the Deputy Commissioner of the Santal Paraganas, for kindly permitting me to utilise their unpublished records. I am thankful to the Librarian of the Imperial Library, Calcutta, for his issuing to me on loan copies of 'The Friend of India' and 'The Calcutta Review.' I express with thanks my obligation to Mr. G. E. Fawcus, M.A., I.E.S., C.I.E., O.B.E., Chairman, Joint Public Service Commission, Ranchi, to Dr. H. Lambert, M.A., Ph.D., I.E.S., ex-Principal, Patna College, to Mr. J. S. Armour, M.A., I.E.S., Director of Public Instruction, Bihar, to Dr. S. C. Sarkar, M.A., D.Phil. (Oxon.), Head of the Department of History, Patna College, and to my revered Professors of Calcutta University, Dr. S. N. Sen, B.Litt. (Oxon.), M.A., Ph.D. (now Keeper of Records of the Government of India), Dr. Hemchandra Raychaudhuri, M.A., Ph.D., Dr. N. C. Banerjee, M.A., Ph.D., and Srijut Tripurari Chakravarty, M.A., for help and encouragement that they have all along extended to me in my humble literary pursuits. I owe a heavy debt of gratitude to the authorities of my *Alma Mater*, the University of Calcutta, for having so kindly published this book, as also two others, in their press. My friends Babu Hemendranath Chakravarty of Pakur, Babu Gourihar Mitra, B.L., of Suri, and Babu Radhagobinda Ruj of Panchkethia, deserve my hearty thanks for supplying me with the records No. 3, No. 4 and No. 6 respectively. My friend and pupil, Babu Hariranjan Ghoshal, M.A., B.L., Research Scholar in History, Patna College, has kindly helped me in preparing the index, for which I thank him cordially.

KALIKINKAR DATTA

PATNA COLLEGE, PATNA,
BIHAR.

The Santal Insurrection of 1855-57

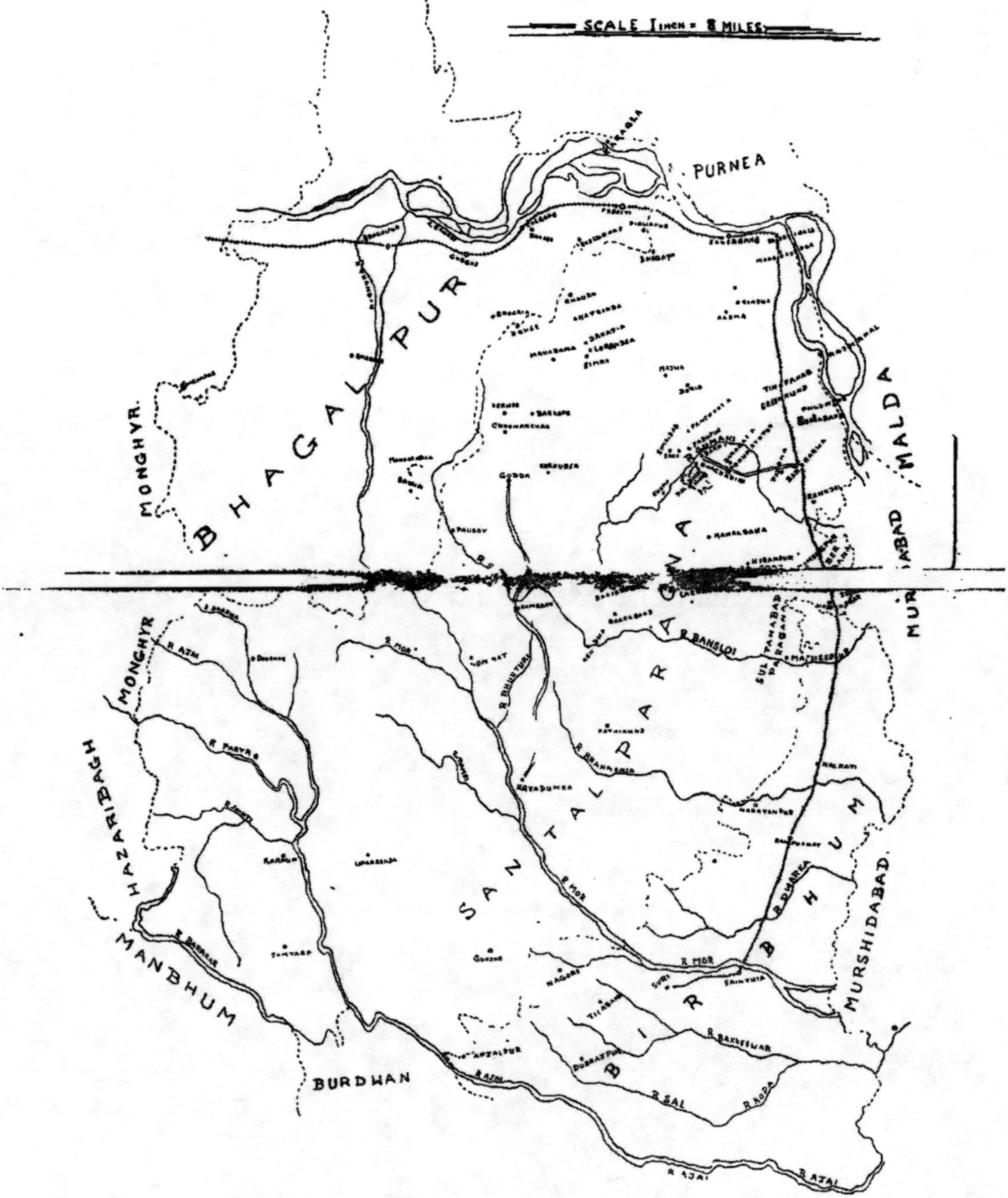

A Sketch map of the district of Santal Parganas and the portions of the Bhagalpur and the Birbhum district showing the places connected with the thesis.

The Santal Insurrection of 1855-57

The Santal Insurrection of 1855-57

CHAPTER I

THE DAMIN-I-KOH AND GENESIS OF THE INSURRECTION

The expansion of the British dominion in India, and the growth of an Indo-British administrative system, naturally conducted India through manifold processes of transition—political, economic, and social. This, for diverse reasons, generated fumes of discontent, among various sections of the people in different parts of India,[1] which burst into flames in the Mutiny of 1857-59. But already, before this wider movement, a considerable insurrection had broken out in the year 1855 in a remote corner of Bengal, now represented by the Bihar district of the Santal Parganas,[2] a part of the Bhagalpur District, and also a portion of the Birbhum District. All these apparently unconnected disturbances were really the manifestations of the adjustment of the country, during about a century, to the new political fact of British dominion and government, and every rising was a test of it, the last great test being the Mutiny.

[1] The Bareilly rising of 1816 due to the mismanagement by native officials of the administration of a newly assessed chaukidari tax; the Cole rising of 1831-32 and other petty risings in Chotanagpur and Palamu (Thornton, *History of the British Empire in India*, Vol. V, pp. 202-04); Muslim risings like the Ferazee disturbances at Barasat in 1831 under the guidance of Syed Ahmad and his disciple Meer Niser Ali or Tittoo Mir (Thornton, *op. cit.*, Vol. V, pp. 178-88) and later in 1847 at Faridpur under the leadership of their descendant Deedoo Meer (Calcutta Review, 1556); and the Moplah outbreaks in August, 1849, in 1851, in 1852 and in September, 1855 (Lee Warner, *Life of Lord Dalhousie*, Vol. II, pp. 57-59).

[2] The major portion of this area was indeed a most important and integral part of Bengal during the greater part of the 18th century and in the preceding few centuries. *Vide* Appendix A.

The Santals in the Damin-i-koh

The Santals immigrated in large numbers into the area called the *Damin-i-koh*,[3] or skirts of the Rajmahal Hills, during the second half of the 18th century and the early 19th century, from Cuttack, Dhalbhum, Manbhum, Barabhum, Chotanagpur, Palamu, Hazaribagh, Midnapur, Bankura, and Birbhum.[4] Through their own industry, and also under encouragement from Lord William Bentinck's government, they cleared the forests, covering the plains extending from the base of the Rajmahal Hills, and brought large tracts of land under cultivation,[5] in spite of the opposition of the local *pahariahs* (earlier original inhabitants of the Hills distinct from the Bengalees living in the plains below).[6] There the Santals, unacquainted with conventionalities and 'trickeries'[7] led simple lives with profuse necessary requirements.[8]

Formation of the Damin-i-koh : Its Administration and Economic Condition

The *Damin-i-koh*, formed in 1832-33 within a definite boundary, demarcated by Mr. John Petty Wood, of the Civil Service, in company with Captain Tanner as Surveyor, was

[3] 'Notes upon the Geology of the Rajmahal Hills' by Thomas Oldham in *Journal of the Asiatic Society of Bengal*, 1854, pp. 263-82.

[4] Dalton, *Descriptive Ethnology of Bengal* (1872), p. 208 Mr. Sutherland's Report to the Secretary to Government, Fort William, on the Hill people (copy preserved in the Record office of the Deputy Commissioner of Santal Parganas). A very valuable and interesting account of the Santals, and their immigration into the Damin-i-koh and the Rajmahal Hills, has been left by Captain Walter S Sherwill, who was employed in the Government Revenue Survey of the Bihar Province and carried out his revenue survey of this part in 1846-50 A.D. It was published in J.A.S.B , 1851 A.D.

[5] Sutherland Report, Calcutta Review, 1856

[6] We get accounts of the *pahariahs* in *Asiatic Researches*, Vol. IV, pp. 45-107, Hamilton Buchanan's *Bhagalpur Journal* in J.B.O.R.S., Sept.-Dec., 1929 and Bishop Heber's *Narrative of a Journey through the Upper Provinces of Hindusthan*, Vol. I, Chapter IX.

[7] Calcutta Review, 1856.

[8] J.A.S.B., 1851, p. 548.

distributed among the districts of Bhagalpur, Murshidabad, and Birbhum. It comprised 1366·01 square miles, of which the space not occupied by the hills was 500 square miles. Of the latter, 246 square miles "were in the survey of 1850 still covered with jungle," the rest or 254 miles being cleared. For fiscal and general civil affairs, it was since 1837-38 under a Superintendent, named Mr. James Pontet of the uncovenanted Civil Service, who was required "to guard the interest of the Government by making favourable land-settlements with the Santals and to collect the rent," [9] and was responsible to the Commissioner of Bhagalpur. In 1838 the annual ground rent of the *Damin-i-koh* amounted to 2,000 rupees and the number of Santal villages to nearly 40 "with a population of about three thousand souls." [9a] But by 1851 Mr. Pontet raised the annual rent to Rs. 43,918-13-5½, and the number of Santals, who were "induced to immigrate into the valleys and into the *Damin-i-koh*," increased to 82,795 souls living in 1,473 villages, of which only 1,164 paid rent.[9b] For criminal matters, it was under the Magistrate of Bhagalpur and *thanas* (police-stations) were attached to Bhagalpur, Berhampore, and Birbhum. There was only one local Magistrate at Deoghur, [10] and most of the people had to go to Bhagalpur, Birbhum, or Aurangabad (then a subdivision of Berhampore) for justice. The Superintendent sometimes decided petty cases, but for important ones the Santals had to go to the courts at Bhagalpur. Even by undertaking a troublesome journey to the Court of Justice, situated at a considerable distance from his home, a Santal could not always expect justice because of the various artifices practised by the cunning *amlahs*, *mukhteers*, *peons*, and *barkandazes*. Further, while "he found justice in the shape of the Magistrate so

[9] *Ibid.*

[9a] *Ibid.*

[9b] *Ibid.*

[10] Calcutta Review, 1860

far off and so terribly difficult of access, he found justice nearer home in the shape of the Darogahs and Thannah police, the authorised agents of the District Magistrate, but found it only to find it his bane." [11]

The plains lying below the Hills, originally belonging to the Bengal *subah* of the Mughal Empire, were inhabited for a long time by Bengalis.[11a] Gradually, more Bengali families of *moirā*, *beniā*, and other castes, coming from the districts of Burdwan and Birbhum, and also a number of Bhojpuris and Bhattiyas,[12] that is, up-country merchants coming from Shahabad, Chuprah, Bettiah, Arrah, and some other places, settled within the jurisdiction of the *Damin-i-koh* being attracted by the facilities available there for trade and money-lending business.[13] Barhait (situated about 13 miles N.W. of the Barharwa Ry. Station, E.I.Ry. Loop), "the capital town of the Hills," was (in 1851) "a substantial village with a large population and about 50 families of Bengali traders" ; there was a good *bazar* there, where two markets were held a week. There was also a large tank, and Mr. Potent, Superintendent of the *Damin-i-koh*, had planted there a plot of ground with potatoes. From Barhait, large quantities of rice, *borā*, mustard, and several other oil-seeds, were carried on bullock-carts by many Bengali *mahājans* (traders and money-lenders) to Jangipur on the Bhagirathi, from which place these were conveyed to Murshidabad, and eventually to Calcutta, "whence much of the mustard," carried from these hills, was "exported to England."[14] In return for these grains, the Santals were paid in money, salt, tobacco, or cloth. Several Bengali grain-dealers, living at Kathikund (in the Dumka subdivision), bought

11 *Ibid*, and also of 1856

11a *Vide* Appendix A.

12 Karun Record and Panchkethia Record

13 I have studied these facts by touring through the interior places of the district of Santal Parganas

14 J A S B , 1851, pp 574-76

mustard-seeds and rice from the Santals, "but for a price far below its true value."[15] They exported these grains to Suri.[16]

Genesis of the Insurrection

The insurrection of 1855 was not a mere spasmodic outburst of the crude instincts of the semi-savage Santals. In fact, wrote Captain Sherwill in 1851, the Santals were "in general an orderly race of people, their rulers have little more to do than bear their honours and collect the rent."[17] The causes of the insurrection were deeply rooted in the changing conditions of the time. It had its origin in the economic grievances of the Santals, due to the oppressions and frauds committed on those simple-minded people by the above-mentioned Bengali and up-country merchants and money-lenders. The extortions of those merchants and *mahājans* had become awful, and they had amassed large fortunes within an incredibly short period by securing cash and grains from the Santals through various obnoxious ways.[18] They lent a few rupees, some rice, or other articles to the Santals during the rainy season, and "thus became the arbiters of their fate and held in hand their destiny throughout life."[19] On the approach of the harvest season, those money-lenders set out on their annual tours of collection with bullock-carts and horses. They picked up a stone on the way, and having painted it with vermilion to show the correctness of its weight, arrived at the farms of their debtors, who had then to provide for the boarding expenses of their creditors' parties. By weighing with the help of the aforesaid piece of stone, the *mahājans* took away almost the whole produce of the lands of their debtors, still leaving them overburdened with debts. Further,

15 *Ibid*, p. 566.

16 *Ibid.*

17 *Ibid.*

18 Pakur Record. Definite instances have been given in the Calcutta Review of 1856.

19 Pakur Record.

those money-lenders kept two sets of weighing scales—(1) *Kenārām* or *Bara Bau*, the capacity of which was a little more than that of the ordinary measure and which was used by them for weighing the crops that they took from their debtors, and (2) *Bechārām* or *Chota Bau*, the value of which was below that of the standard measure and which was used for weighing articles lent to the Santals by them.[20] They also charged extraordinarily high rates of interest. A Santal "saw his crops, his cattle, even himself and family appropriated for a debt which ten times paid remained an incubus upon him still."[21] Barhait and Hiranpur (situated 14 miles to the west of Pakur) were the two important centres, where thus sprang up a class of rich money-lenders at the cost of the interests of the Santals. In short, from the time that those merchants from the outside had "taken up their abode in the hills, the condition of the Santals had undergone a gradual but serious change."[22] To add to the misfortunes of the Santals, "the greedy Zamindars living near the borders of the Damin had began for some time to cast a wistful eye" on their lands.[23] We find the follwing passage in the *Calcutta Review* of 1856 illustrating this point :—

"Gangadhar is an influential zemindar. The border of his Tuppeh touches the boundary pillars (of the Damin) ; within the pillars Manick Santhal has a lovely spot of corn-land which he has nourished with frugal care ; he has paid his rent for it for five years ; Gangadhar can by no means claim it, for even his own ancestor has signed that plot away. As, however, Manick has paid six annas per mensem for the ground, he or his Gomasta thinks no harm of levying from him the lenient sum of 6 rupees in consideration of the fact that he will thenceforth be relieved of his exactions for that year."[24] Mr. W. C. Taylor,

20 *Ibid.*
21 Calcutta Review, 1860.
22 Calcutta Review, 1856, p 238
23 *Ibid.*
24 *Ibid*, p. 240.

Assistant Commissioner at Sreekoond (near Tinpahar), wrote to Mr. A. R. Thompson, Deputy Commissioner at Naya Dumka, on the 16th of February, 1856, that the Rajahs of Mahespur and Pakur were hated by the Santals because they granted leases of Santal villages to the non-Santals.[25] Further, the police were "base and corrupt," [26] the "higher grades as well as the lower, with a few bright and honourable exceptions, preying upon the people and making unlawful gains."[27] The law courts were full of *amlahs* or officers, not less given to illicit gains of a like nature.[28] The *Naib Suzawals*,[29] who collected rents from the *Parganaits*, the *Manjhis*,[30] and the innocent Santal peasants, were generally guilty of committing terrible oppressions on them and "where authorized to receive some six rupees on behalf of the Sircar (government), they will lay some six other rupees for their private benefit ; or where a rent of 4 annas for a plot and all it contained was fixed in the settlement, they take a rupee more for a sapling bamboo clump, or a solitary fruit tree, growing thereon." [31] At the time of his trial, Kanhu, one of the leaders of the insurrection, expressed openly that Mahesh Datta, *Daroga* or *Naib Suzawal* of Dighee, and Kali Prasad, *Naib Suzawal* of Tekree (Rajmahal) or Sukree (Sakrigali), 'took bribes and were hated by the Santals.'[32] Thus, as it has been graphically described by a contemporary writer, "Zamindars—or more properly speaking Zamindari retainers, as gomasta, surbarakar, peons and other mahajuns and their 'mustajirs' or agents—the police, the revenue and court amlas have exercised a combined system of

25 Record Room of the Deputy Commissioner of Santal Paraganas

26 Calcutta Review, 1856

27 *Ibid.*

28 *Ibid*

29 There were four *Naib Suzawals* to assist the Superintendent in collecting rent and settling disputes about lands

30 J A S.B., 1851, p. 554 *Manjhi*=a village headman *Parganait*=the head of a number of villages and generally also a village headman

31 Calcutta Review, 1856

32 Letter from Mr W. C. Taylor to Mr. A R, Thompson at Naya Dumka, dated the 28th February, 1856, para 9

extortions, oppressive exactions, forcible dispossession of property, abuse and personal violence and a variety of petty tyrannies upon the timid and yielding Santals. Usurious interest on loans of money ranging from 50 to 500 per cent.; false measures at the *haut* and market; wilful and uncharitable trespass by the rich by means of their untethered cattle, tattoos, ponies, and even elephants, on the growing crops of the poorer race; and such like illegalities have been prevalent. Even a demand by individuals from the Santals of security for good conduct is a thing not unknown; embarrassing pledges for debt also formed another mode of oppression."[33] The Santals issued a manifesto in the *Kythe* (a form of Hindi) language at Bhagalpur and Purneah on the 10th of Srāvaṇa, 1262 B.S. or 25th July, 1855 A.D. It set forth that the "sin of the Muhajun (*Mahājan*), and of the amlah, is great and that the Sahebs delegate the duty of investigation to subordinate officers who oppress them, and have produced their change of character and action."[34] Lastly, the Europeans employed in Railway construction works also occasionally oppressed the Santals. The *Calcutta Review* of 1856 notes a case of "alleged forcible abduction of two Santal women, and even murder, and some unjust acts of oppression, as taking kids, fowl, etc., without payment on the part of Europeans employed on the line of the railroad."

The discontent among the Santals of the *Damin-i-koh* was shared, though in a less degree, by their brethren in places to the south and west of that tract, and vague allusions were made to one Morgo Rajah, who, as a Santal chief living near the Pareshnath Hills, had, it was said, imposed upon himself the task of organising the Santals of the south in an independent

[33] Calcutta Review, 1856.

[34] *Ibid.* Compare: "Among the Judges, Collectors, and Magistrates in the Mofussil there are many who place much confidence in their Amlas, who for that reason become bold in the exercise of power, and the consequence is that their situations turn into streams of corruption in which they bathe and become happy but it at once lowers the reputation of their superior officers ....."—Quoted from the Bengali Journal *Bhāskar* of the 15th of March, 1842, in the *Bengal Spectator* of April, 1842.

kingdom.[35] There was also a story, which connected the Santal insurrection with Meer Abbas Ali, the ex-Amir of Sind, who had then come to Hazaribagh on a hunting excursion. The Amir was unjustly charged by one Arjoon Manjhi with having incited the Santals to rise in insurrection. It was an entirely false charge against the Amir, who, like others of his race, was passionately fond of hunting and maintained, during his residence at Hazaribagh, a "large hunting establishment for which he had then collected the Santals from Ramgurh, Khurruckdeah, Deoghur, and from some of the villages of the Bhagalpur and Birbhum districts." Mr. J. Allen, the then Commissioner of Chotanagpur, conducted a "careful enquiry" regarding this charge against the Amir, and wrote a letter[36] to Mr. Grey, Secretary to the Government of Bengal, on the 17th December, 1855, wherein he expressed: "After a careful enquiry I have arrived at the conclusion, that Meer Abbas Ali Khan has not had anything to do with this insurrection." The Santals of Hazaribagh might have sympathised with their brethren of the Bhagalpur and the Birbhum district and reinforced their numbers and strength, but there is no reason to believe that the ex-Amir of Sind did anything to fan the flame of their discontent or countenance their activities.

Oppressions seldom go unresisted, and economic troubles very often cause the outburst of smouldering discontent. The Santals, gradually realising the causes of their increasing debts and poverty, sought a redress for their grievances by striking at the root of all these. In fact, shortly before the outbreak of the insurrection, the *Parganaits* and *Manjhis* of different villages "seem to have begun in right earnest to cogitate what might be the proper course for them to pursue."[37] Thus the movement was the product of a "long course of oppression

35 Calcutta Review, 1856.

36 D C Record Room. *Vide* Appendix A for a full text of it.

37 Calcutta Review, 1856; Pakur Record.

silently and patiently submitted to by those unsophisticated people, unaccustomed to fight for their own rights in the legitimate ways with their neighbours.''[38]

Original Character of the Movement Not Anti-British

The movement was not anti-British in the beginning; but it was directed chiefly against the *mahājans* and traders. The Santals at first declared that their new God had directed them to collect and pay revenue to the State at the rate of two annas on every buffalo-plough, and half an anna on each cow-plough per annum. The rate of interest was to be one pice in a rupee a year.[39] Gradually, however, the nature of the movement changed, as the insurgents directed their attacks against the oppressive *Naib Suzawals*, the police, and the courts then working under the Company Raj. The Santals were further exasperated, when those among them, who had made night-attacks on the houses of some of the *mahājans*, were "tried and punished," while "their oppressors (*the mahājans*) were not even rebuked."[40] Thus their attacks against the officers of the Company, and other activities, obstructed for a few months the peaceful consolidation of British rule in the *Damin-i-koh* and the surrounding areas.

Signs of Disorder in 1854

It has been already noted that signs of disorder had appeared and the chief Santals had begun to talk about their grievances among themselves in the year 1854. Some among them tried to rob the *mahājans* of their ill-earned wealth by "dacoities, burglaries and theft,"[41] which were, writes a contemporary account, "well-merited reprisals for their unprovoked cruelties."[42] A detailed account of these has been left by the late Babu

[38] Pakur Record. [39] Calcutta Review, 1856. [40] *Ibid.*

[41] Letter from the Commissioner of Bhagalpur to the Secretary to the Government of Bengal, dated the 9th July, 1855, para 4.

[42] Calcutta Review, 1856.

Digambar Chakravarty, a pleader of Pakur.[43] One day, early in the year 1854, Bir Singh, *Parganait* of Sasan in Lachimpur, declared that their principal God, Chando Bonga, having appeared before him, inspired him with some magical charms, through which he could cause the sound sleep of any man whom he wished to rob of his wealth. Thus he formed a powerful gang of many followers, prominent among whom were Bir Singh Manjhi of Borio,[44] Kaoleh Paramanik of Sindree, and Doman Manjhi of Hatbanda in Lachmipur. They committed robberies in the houses of Isree Bhakat and Tilak Bhakat of Litipara, Jitu Kolhu (oil-man) of Bagsisa, and in several houses at Dariapur.[45] The *moirās* and other *dikus* (the Bengalees were so termed by the Santals) kept a watch on their movements and enquired of them the reasons for their holding meetings at night. They replied that their nightly meetings were meant for worshipping the God Siva of Gadi,[46] and frustrated all the attempts of the *dikus* to know the secrets of their meetings. The *mahājans* then reported their movements to Mahesh Lal Datta, who held the post of the *Naib Suzawal* or Daroga of *thana* (police-station) Dighee[47] since 1835, and requested him to take prompt measures to check their nefarious activities. The latter at first paid no heed to their request, whereupon they sought the help of Rani Kshemāsundarī, the *zamindar* of Ambar Pargana ('Pakur Raj').[48] Babu Jagabandhu Roy,[49] the then *Diwan* of the Pakur

43 *History of the Santal Hool of 1855.*

44 Twenty miles due west of Rajmahal.

45 Pakur Record.

46 A place of pilgrimage lying 5 miles north of Barhait · many persons flock there during the *Sivaratri* festival.

47 A few miles south of Colgong.

48 The Pakur Raj family has an interesting history. The most famous member of this family was the late Rajah Prithvichand Sahi. Hamilton Buchanan, who saw him at Pakur on the 13th of December, 1810 A.D., thus remarks :" He is a stout, sensible and obliging man, who not only visited me, a civility that very few deign to show, but invited me to visit him. His house is decent, and is gradually enlarging" (J.B.O.R.S., Sept.-Dec., 1929). He was the author of the famous Bengali work named '*Gaurīmangala*' (D. C. Sen, *Baṅgabhāṣā o Sāhitya*). Rani Kshemāsundarī was his daughter-in-law.

49 He was the founder of the Zamindar family of Kinchantala (Dhulian) in the Murshidabad District.

Raj Estate, passed orders on the *Naib* of the Santali *mahals* to look into the matter, but the *Naib* "was a worthless man and was one of those whom the poor Santals hated the most, because instead of helping them in any way he sided with the relentless money-lenders in harassing them."[50] He summoned Bir Singh Manjhi to the Zamindari *kachari*, imposed a heavy fine upon him and demanded its immediate payment. When the latter pleaded innocence and expressed his inability to pay the fine, he was mercilessly beaten with shoes before his followers. These measures highly exasperated Bir Singh and his followers, and goaded them on to the extreme step of committing dacoities on the money-lenders. The *Naib* then requested the *Diwan* to engage some well-trained sepoys with arms, and also some Pathan inhabitants of Samsergang (near Dhulian in the Murshidabad District), to guard the *kachari* house of the Zamindar of Pakur there.

There were some rich *moirās* living at Kusma near Barhait. One night, Bir Singh with his followers broke into the house of one of them, and when the *pahariah* archers employed by the said *mahājans* fled away, his party looted the house and other houses as well. On the following day, the *mahājans* sent a report once again to Mahesh Lal Datta regarding those docoities. The Daroga then proceeded with a batch of constables to arrest the Santal dacoits. He unjustly harassed one rich but innocent Santal named Gocho, brother of one Bhaja Parganait. Gocho had in his possession gold mohurs and silver coins "which they called *Lat Sahi* Taka as much as would fill up eight vats of tolerable capacities."[51] His wealth had excited the lust of the money-lenders, who accused him before the Daroga of theft. Being roughly handled by Mahesh Lal Datta, Gocho expressed before him: "We shall see how much twine could the Daroga procure, so as to fasten all the peaceful Santals whom the wicked Daroga

50 Pakur Record.

51 *Ibid.*

wanted to be sent up." Gocho, or any other member of this party, was not of course arrested immediately by the Daroga, and during that year there was no disturbance. But it was lull before a great storm, which soon appeared in the shape of a formidable insurrection. Early in the following year, on the complaint of the *mahājans,* Mahesh Lal arrested Gocho with many other Santals and inflicted harsh punishments upon them.[12]

Ibid.

CHAPTER II

Outbreak and Progress of the Insurrection

The measures adopted by Mahesh Lal Daroga to suppress the dacoities and other disorders, greatly intensified the discontent of the Santals. So about 6,000 or 7,000 of them came from Birbhum, Bankura, Chotanagpur, and Hazaribagh, early in 1855 A.D., "for the purpose (it was rumoured) of avenging the punishment inflicted on their comrades in the last year's Dacoities. These Dacoitics were committed on the Bengalee Mahajans, who had oppressed them, and they complained that their comrades had been punished while nothing had been done to the Mahajans whose exactions had compelled them to take the law into their own hands."[53] Their endurance had "reached its maximum; and while the spirits of the people were in this condition, it needed but a spark to kindle the fire."[54] This spark came from two brothers named Sidhu and Kanhu of Bhagnadihi, situated half a mile from Barhait, with their less pushing brothers Chand and Bhairab.[55] Religion often acts as a great stimulating force among the average masses; and here also the story of a miraculous divine revelation inspired the Santals to take prompt and open measures for the removal of their distresses. The revelation came all of a sudden. Sidhu and Kanhu "were at night seated in their home, revolving upon many things (in their minds); their brothers, Chand and Bhyrub (Bhairab), were ten miles away at Simulchap; a bit of paper fell on Seedoo's

53 Letter from the Commissioner of Bhagalpur to the Secretary to the Government of Bengal, dated the 9th July, 1855, para. 4.

54 Calcutta Review, 1856.

55 *Ibid.*

(Sidhu's) head, and suddenly the Thakur (God) appeared before the astonished gaze of Seedoo (Sidhu) and Kanhu; he was like a white man though dressed in the native style; on each hand he had ten fingers; he held a white book, and wrote therein; the book and with it 20 pieces of paper, in 5 batches, four in each batch, he presented to the brothers; ascended upwards and disappeared. Another bit of paper fell on Seedoo's head, and then came two men, each having six fingers on each hand; hinted to them the purport of the Thakoor's order, and they likewise vanished. But there was not merely one apparition of the sublime Thakoor; each day in the week. for some short period, did he make known his presence to his favoured apostles; at one time it was in a flame or fire, with a book, some white paper, and knife, at another in the figure of . . . a solid cart-wheel. In the silvery pages of the book, and upon the white leaves of the single scrap of paper, were words written; these were afterwards deciphered by literate Santals, able to read and interpret; but their meaning had already been sufficiently indicated to the two leaders."[56] Sidhu and Kanhu arranged for the proper worship of the Thakur by erecting his figure in the garden enclosure of their house, and in the meanwhile they circulated the mysterious revelation by the symbol of a Sal tree branch.[57] A day was fixed for a gathering of all the Santals to hear the command of their Thakur.

Thus, on the 30th of, June, 1855, about 10,000 Santals met at Bhagnadihi, when the divine order that the Santals should get out of their oppressors' control was announced to them by Sidhu and Kanhu. It has been said that letters were then written by Kirta, Bhadoo and Sunno *Manjhis* at Sidhu's "direction addressed to Government, to the Commissioner, Collector, and Magistrate of Bhagalpur, the Collector and Magistrate of

56 *Ibid.*

57 This practice is still current among the Santals Whenever they want to circulate anything, they do so by carrying branches of Sal tree in the markets and other places.

Birbhum, to the Darogahs of Thannahs Dighee and Tikree (Rajmahal) and to several Zemindars and others; from the Darogahs and Zemindars replies were called for within 15 days."[58] The Santals declared their determination to do away with the Bengali and up-country *mahājans*, to "take possession of the country and set up a Government of their own."[59] Certain castes like *kumars* (potters), *telis*, (oilmen), blacksmiths, *momins* (Muhammadan weavers), *chamars* (shoemakers), and *domes*, who were obedient to the Santals and helped them in several ways, were exempted from their vengeance.[60] The Commissioner of Bhagalpur wrote to the Secretary to the Government of Bengal on the 28th July, 1855: "From all accounts it appears that the Santals are led on and incited to acts of oppression by the Gwallahs (milkmen), telis (oilmen) and other castes who supply them with intelligence, beat their drums, direct their proceedings and act as spies. These people as well as the Lohars (blacksmiths) who make their arrows and axes ought to meet with condign punishment and be speedily included in any proclamation which Government may see fit to issue against the rebels."

On Saturday, the 18th of Āṣāḍh, 1262 B.S., the Santal insurgents proceeded from Bhagnadihi to the neighbouring *bazar* at Panchkethia with the object of propitiating a local goddess,[61] much venerated by the people there, before commencing their adventure.[62]

Their movements caused immense anxiety in the minds of the *mahājans* of that bazar. Five of them, Manik Chowdhry, Gorachand Sen, Sarthak Rakshit, Nimai Datta, and Hiru Datta were mercilessly killed by them. Mahesh Lal Datta, *Daroga* of *thana* Dighee, reached that place on the 7th

58 Calcutta Review, 1856.

59 *Ibid*.- Karun Record; Panchkethia Record.

60 *Ibid*.

61 *Ibid*.

62 *Ibid*.

July, 1855, with his party. But he was soon killed by Sidhu along with a few others (19 persons in all), such as a *mahājan*, two *barkandazes* (armed retainers) and some *chowkidars* (village watchmen).[63] Of the four leaders, Chand was absent from that place. Two men, a *barkandaz* and a *pyada* (a sepoy), who had been present with the Daroga when the latter was killed but had fortunately escaped to return to their station, gave out that the Santal chiefs "received the Daroga at first in a civil manner and allowed him to sit alone with him; but taunted him with having come to apprehend them, dared him to do so, told him he had better send troops and they then required him to levy a tax of 5 rupees on each Bengalee and deliver them up to their mercy. The Daroga . . . behaved with much temper and discretion, endeavouring to pacify them; assuring them he would try to comply with their wishes as far as lies in his power and advising them to disperse quietly and cultivate their fields so that they might be able to pay their rents. The Daroga then rose to come away when all of a sudden the order was given by the youngest of the four brothers to seize and beat."[64] They themselves "contrived to make their escape after being knocked about and wounded but not before the Daroga, two Burkundazes and 5 or 6 more had their heads cut off."[65] The Santals thus wreaked vengeance on Mahesh Lal Datta, for his having suppressed the dacoities of the year 1854 with strong but unwise measures,[66] by murdering him brutally. Pertabnarain, *Naib Suzawal* of *thana* Kurhurrea (in the Godda subdivision), who had been for some time absent on

[63] Letter from the Commissioner of Bhagalpur to the Secretary to the Government of Bengal, dated the 9th July, 1855, para. 3.

[64] Letter from the Commisoioner of Bhagalpur to the Secretary to the Government of Bengal, dated the 10th July, 1855, para. 2.

[65] *Ibid.*

[66] Pakur Record. Letter from the Junior Secretary to the Government of Bengal to the Commissioner of Bhagalpur, dated Darjeeling, the 11th March, 1856 (copy preserved in the Commissioner's office at Bhagalpur).—Calcutta Review, 1856.

leave but had to join his service owing to the Santal outbreak, ordered one Sulkhun Parganait to "adopt measures to prevent the insurrection, but not finding him, he was returning to the Thanah when he met an assembly of Santals who first took him off to Sonar Chuck (Choona Chak near Kerwar in the Godda subdivision) saying the Thakur had called him and then there murdered him."[67]

The insurgents soon plundered the Barhait *bazar*, which was then (as is also now) full of many rich *mahājans*, and thence marched in different directions with bows, poisoned arrows, axes, and swords, and committing plunders and atrocities on their way. For fear of life, the Bengali and Hindusthani inhabitants of those places took to their heels, leaving their hearth and home behind.[68] While proceeding from Babupur to Panchkethia, Kanhu killed one Khan Saheb, a local *Naib Suzawal*.[69]

Intervention of the Bhagalpur and Damin Officers

Thus, the movement of the Santals soon proved to be a menace to public peace and order, creating a general panic, and the attention of the Company's Government was necessarily drawn towards its suppression. It "came like a thunder-clap upon those who heard of it, that in the centre of Bengal there was a rebellion and that a race of people, almost unheard and certainly unthought of, were in arms, murdering and running riot"[70] throughout the land. "Such a strange occurrence," remarked a writer in the *Calcutta Review* of 1855, "has not clouded the prosperity of the Lower Provinces of Bengal within the Anglo-Indian memory of man." On the 4th of July, 1855, Mr. H. E. Richardson, the then officiating Magistrate of Bhagalpur,

[67] Letter from the Magistrate of Bhagalpur to the Commissioner of Bhagalpur, dated 17th January, 1857.

[68] Panchkethia Record; Karun Record.

[69] Calcutta Review, 1856.

[70] Calcutta Review, 1860.

received a report about the outbreak of the insurrection. The "report seemed so strange and unlikely that at first little credit was attached to it."[71] But it being repeated the next day, Mr. H. E. Richardson and Mr. Pontet, Superintendent of the *Damin-i-koh*, proceeded to Rajmahal, where they arrived in the evening of the 6th of July.[72] Mr. C. F. Brown, the Commissioner of Bhagalpur, received two reports about the disturbances in the afternoon of the 8th July, one (dated 7th July) from the *mohurir* (clerk) of the *thana* at Borio, and the other (dated 5 A.M. of 8th July) from the Post-office overseer of that place.[73] He immediately requested Major F. W. Burroughs [74] "to despatch a force to Rajmahal for the purpose of quelling the disturbance; the insurgents having given out that they intended to attack that place." But on receiving information, in the morning of the 9th July, that the insurgents, after having plundered several villages between Borio and Colgong, were moving in the direction of Bhagalpur as well as in that of Rajmahal, and that they had in fact arrived within 20 miles of the latter place, he modified his former orders, and asked Major Burroughs to arrange for sending a detachment to Rajmahal and also to be careful "to reserve a force sufficient for the defence" of Bhagalpur, if necessary.[75] He further "issued orders to the Hill Sirdars, to the Zamindars of the neighbouring Pergunnahs (*parganas*) and the neighbouring Darogahs for aid in suppressing the insurrection" and "obtained the loan of hundred muskets from Major Burroughs with the view of arming the town Police," as the Santal prisoners in the Bhagalpur jail (under sentence of transportation) had given out that the "station will be attacked" [76] and the inhabitants

71 Letter from the Commissioner of Bhagalpur to the Secretary to the Government of Bengal, dated the 9th July, 1855, para. 1.

72 *Ibid.*

73 *Ibid*, para. 3.

74 Letters to Major Burroughs from the Commissioner of Bhagalpur, dated the 8th July and the 9th July, 1855.

75 *Ibid*, para. 6.

76 Same as f. n. 71, para. 6.

had "in consequence been afraid with panic."[77] Apprehending disturbance of the postal communications between Bhagalpur and Rajmahal, he sent a duplicate of his letter, dated the 9th July, 1855, to the Secretary to the Government of Bengal in Calcutta, *via* Patna. The *dak chowkis* (postal stations) between Bhagalpur and Monghyr were disturbed,[78] and the *dak* runners abandoned the road between Bhagalpur and Colgong, though there were no reasons for that, as the communications in that direction had remained till then unimpeded.[79] There were, however, good grounds for believing that the *dak* line through the Hills, *via* Borio to Rajmahal, was infested with insurgent Santals, "who would stop the dawk if sent that way," and therefore the Commissioner of Bhagalpur wrote to the Postmaster there on the 11th July, 1855, that "he should adopt immediate measures for having the dwak (as it formerly used to be) through Colgong and Sicree (Sakrigali) to Rajmahal," as he believed that there was no "reason for apprehension of its being intercepted along that line of road." No *dak* from Rajmahal had reached Bhagalpur since the 8th July.[80]

While at Rajmahal, Mr. Richardson and Mr. Pontet borrowed, on the 9th July, 1855, some *cutlasses* and boarding *pikes* from the Captain of the steamer 'Meghna,' which had been passing by that way, with the object of defending themselves, in case that place was attacked.[81] Mr. Barnes, an indigo-planter at Colgong,[82] wrote to the Commissioner of Bhagalpur in the morning of the 11th July, 1855, that there

77 *Ibid*

78 Letter from the Commissioner of Bhagalpur to the Secretary to the Government of Bengal, dated 10th July, 1855, 9 P.M.

79 *Ibid.*

80 Letter from same to same, dated 12th July, 1855, para. 4.

81 *Ibid*, dated 11th July, 1855.

82 The factory house of Mr. Barnes later on passed into the possession of the Ganguli Zamindars of Colgong, who have carefully preserved the old building (at a distance of 3 minutes' walk from the local Railway Station) with various decorations and furniture.

was a general rising and "indiscriminate plunder of the villages in that quarter,"[83] and the Thanadar of Colgong also informed him on the same day that the Santals "appearing yesterday afternoon in force at Pyalapoor (Pyalapur, a large village on the high road, eleven miles east of Colgong) the Jamadar of that chowky (*chowki*) had deserted that post."[84] In fact, there was "a general panic" throughout that region and the people were "fleeing in all directions."

The panic increased from day to day.[85] The Commissioner of Bhagalpur wrote to the Secretary to the Government of Bengal on the 10th July, 1855, soliciting the sanction of the Government "for offering a reward of 110 (? 500) rupees for the apprehension of each of the Thakoors or chiefs engaged in this bloody business." Major Burroughs, with 160 rank and file, marched for Rajmahal in the evening of the 10th July, 1858. He could not proceed through the water-passage for want of boats.[86] On reaching Colgong in the morning of the 11th July, he wrote to the Commissioner of Bhagalpur: "We hear that the insurgents move about in very small parties but on their drums sounding they assemble in parties of 10,000 men each for the purpose of plundering and as my detachment is too small to be divided without greatly impairing its efficiency, I think it best to keep in one party ready to oppose any parties I may hear of in this neighbourhood or to intercept their proceeding to Bhagalpur, or move to that station for its defence before they can reach it, should the latter measure appear necessary. As a further rise of the river to the extent of three or four feet (and now it is rising) would place the road between this place and Bhagalpur under water, I think it right to draw your attention to this point when favouring me with your further instructions.

83 Letter from the Commissioner of Bhagalpur to the Government of Bengal, dat d 11th July, 1855.

84 *Ibid.*

85 *Ibid.*

86 *Ib'd*, dated 10th July, 1855.

If the river continues to rise for another week or ten days, it will, I fear, be impassable for troops.

"*P. S.*—As the insurgents are said to move in scattered parties, it seems to me that it would not be prudent for my detachment to move from this place in search of them." [87]

At 10 P.M., on the same date, the Commissioner of Bhagalpur wrote to the officer commanding the troops at Dinapore to send additional troops "to aid Major Burroughs in quelling the insurrection and for the protection" of Bhagalpur. At the same time, he wrote to Mr. C. E. Chapman, Assistant to the Magistrate of Bhagalpur, that Major Burroughs was likely to fall in engagement with the Santals at Pyalapur on the 12th July, and that as "in every expedition of this kind troops are required to act under the orders of the Civil power," and Mr. Richardson was absent from Bhagalpur, he should "proceed with all expedition to Major Burroughs' camp and exercise the authority in question till Mr. Richardson can join." Mr. Chapman received the following instructions from the Commissioner: "Your first duty will of course be to endeavour to pacify and conciliate the Santals by every means in your power; assuring them of favour and protection if they will only conduct themselves in a peaceable manner and of redress and justice should they have any cause of grievance. Force may have the effect of only irritating them still further and should therefore be had recourse to as a...... (not legible) resort." The Commissioner of Bhagalpur wrote to Mr. Richardson also on the 12th July to join Major Burroughs' camp at Pyalapur. He further thought it necessary to correspond with the Magistrates of Birbhum, Bankura, Chotanagpur, Singhbhum, Hazaribagh, Purneah, and Monghyr, on the subject of suppressing the insurrection,[88] and the officiating Magistrate of Bhagalpur wrote immediately to the Magistrate of Berhampore for military aid.

[87] Quoted in *ibid*, dated the 12th July, 1855, 4 P.M.

[88] *Ibid*, para. 5.

• The Commissioner of Bhagalpur came to know from Major Burroughs, through the latter's letter, dated the 13th July, 1855, that he had proceeded beyond Colgong but that he did not think it prudent to " move more than 10 or twelve miles forward until the station of Bhagalpur is better protected." He then informed the Major that " this object (defence of Bhagalpur) will be very shortly effected,"[89] as the Magistrate of Monghyr had already sent there his guard of 38 rank and file and five officers (consisting of 1 Soobadar, 2 Havildars, 2 Naiks) and as also further relief was expected by the arrival of troops from Dinapore in 3 or 4 days. He assured him that he need not be under any apprehension about the attack of Bhagalpur by the insurgents, before it was prepared for defence, and hoped that even if they attempted " to do so they will find it difficult to get across the Ghoga and Chundan Nallas as the Police have charge of the only ghats by which they can come across." [90] He further instructed him thus: " In my opinion, there is no occasion for you to circumscribe your movements on account of any necessity likely to arise for your retracing your steps in order to defend Bhagalpur. And I therefore hope you will proceed in the direction of Pyalapoor (Pyalapur) as soon as possible and check the outrages which are being perpetrated in that vicinity. Orders have already been issued to procure elephants for your detachment but I am sorry to say I have as yet been able to obtain only one and the promise of two others." [91]

Being eager to reinforce the troops under Major Burroughs, the Commissioner of Bhagalpur requested the Magistrate of Purneah, through his letter, dated the 14th July, 1855, to substitute, as soon as possible, *barkandazes* for the Sepoys of the Purneah Guards, to send the latter to help Major Burroughs " with all practicable despatch," and also to send

89 Letter from the Commissioner of Bhagalpur to Major Burroughs, Commanding Hill Rangers, Camp Colgong, dated the 14th July, 1855, 7 A.M.

90 *Ibid.*

91 *Ibid.*

as many elephants as might be necessary not only for the troops that he would send but also ten or twelve more for the use of Major Burroughs' detachment, as the rainy season rendered "it impossible for the men to march without elephants to carry their tents and baggage." The Collector of Purneah was also written to, on the same day, to act in co-operation with the Magistrate of Purneah in the matter of sending help, to note down the names of the elephants, their owners, and *mahuts* (elephant-drivers), as the Government wanted to pay the cost of hiring the elephants, and to send the Sepoys "with a good supply of provisions," which they were not likely to get on this side of the Ganges because the Santals "had been plundering" all the country between Pirpainti and Pyalapur.

In fact, the movement had assumed "a formidable aspect" by the middle of July, 1855, and the insurgents had "commenced murdering the inhabitants."[92] They had an encounter, on the 13th of July, in a village close to Pirpainti, with 6 or 8 men of the Railway staff,[93] who were defeated, three of them being wounded.[94] *Dak* (postal communications) and all "railway operations" between Bhagalpur and Rajmahal had been stopped, and the high road between Pirpainti and Sakrigali had been infested by the insurgents, who had been murdering men, women, and children. Eye-witnesses, who had escaped from those outrages, asserted that "the insurgents loudly boast that the Company's rule is at an end and the regime of their Soobah has commenced."[95] Kishujewan Singh, Thanadar of Dumka, reported before the Commissioner at Bhagalpur that, on his way from Dumka to Bhagalpur, he had seen, on the 13th of

92 Letter from the Commissioner of Bhagalpur to the Commanding Officer at Dinapore, dated the 15th July, 1855.

93 It should be noted that the East India Company's Government had then undertaken the work of extending the Railways through this part of the country.

94 Letter from the Commissioner of Bhagalpur to Major-General Lloyd, Commanding at Dinapore, dated the 17th July, 1855, 10 P.M., para. 7.

95 Letter from the Commissioner of Bhagalpur to the Secretary to the Government of Bengal, dated the 15th July, 1855, para. 4.

July 500 Santals assembled at Kathikund and 400 at Pakrapara, that in passing between Kendowa and Purgadee (at a distance of three miles from Kendowa) on the next day he had seen there about 1,500 of them and that in the afternoon of the same day he had seen 1,000 of them being gathered together in one place between Kowayane and Dhoomputtra. Chittrapat Singh, *diwan* of the Rani of Barkope (in the Godda subdivision), also reported before the Commissioner that he had seen on the 14th and the 15th of July about 1,500 Santals being assembled together at a place between Amdeha and Chunkhalee.[96]

Major Burroughs wrote to the Commissioner of Bhagalpur on the 14th of July, 1855: "At this season men are on furlough and possibly one Regiment from Dinapore might not be sufficient to put down the insurgents on this side of the Damin-i-koh, considering the extensive tract of country they occupy,—its jungly nature, bad roads and determination of the insurgents to fight as in the affair of yesterday with the Europeans and I should therefore be glad to learn your opinion as to whether your views are for at once putting down the insurgents by force or by holding the road between Bhagalpur and Rajmahal clear from their intrusion till after the Rains and then proceeding to force them into submission in the meantime trying conciliation means... ....it seems to me that such force as can be divided in five or six parties of 400 or 500 men will be required for the work in checking the Rajmahal side of the Damin." Mr. C. E. Chapman also noted in his letter to the Commissioner, written on the same date, that the 150 men he had with him were "a mere handful in the country," and requested that a body of troops or two of Irregular Cavalry, stationed at Segowlee, should be sent to reinforce his party. So, the Commissioner again wrote to the Commanding officer at Dinapore on the 15th July, 1855, requesting him for speedy help and

96 Letter from the Commissioner of Bhagalpur to Major-General Lloyd, Commanding Officer at Dinapore, dated the 21st July, 1855.

wrote also to the Secretary to the Government of Bengal on the same day soliciting his permission to take recourse to strong measures ("nothing less than the introduction of martial law"), in order to bring the insurgents "to their senses." He replied to the letter of Mr. C. E. Chapman on the 16th July informing him that he had received news on that day from Major-General Lloyd, Commanding at Dinapore, to the effect that Headquarters of the 40th Regiment N. I. consisting of 500 rank and file and a full complement of officers (9 European officers, 2 European Sergeants, 1 Indian Sergeant, 10 Indian officers, 30 Havildars, 10 Drummers) under Major Shuckburgh had started from Dinapore and was proceeding towards Bhagalpur on steamer. About the plan that was to be followed under the circumstances then prevailing, he recommended the following one to Mr. Chapman: "The troops should proceed to the nearest point where the insurgents are to be found. On your meeting with them if they do not immediately lay down their arms on being called to do so, the troops may at once attack them; if found in the act of murder or pillage they may without parley be treated as rebels." He himself at the same time adopted several measures for the defence of Bhagalpur.[97]

The troops under Major Burroughs were defeated in a fierce engagement with a body of armed Santals near Pirpainti at about 2 P.M. on the 16th July, 1855. "The rebels stood their ground firmly and shot not only with hand-bows but with bows which they used with their feet sitting on the ground to pull them and fought also with a kind of battle-axe. The result was that the Quarter-Master-Sergeant Mr. Braddon (a gentleman belonging to the Railway), some Native officers, and about 25 Sepoys were killed. The party then retired to Pyntee (Pirpainti), where they got on board boats and proceeded up towards Colgong."[98] Mr. G. A. Pepper, Magistrate of Purneah, had come

97 Letter from the Commissioner to Lieut. W. F. Fagan, Commanding the station at Bhagalpur, dated the 16th July, 1855.

98 Letter from the Commissioner of Bhagalpur to Major-General Lloyd, Commanding at Dinapore, dated the 17th July, 1855, 10 P.M., para. 6.

with 58 men of the Hill Rangers to Carragolah with the object of crossing over to Pirpainti, but, on hearing of the reverses of Major Burroughs' troops, sent them on boats to Colgong.[99]

Major Shuckburgh arrived at Bhagalpur with a portion of the 40th Regiment N. I. in the morning of the 17th July by the steamer 'Meghna,' and the rest of it reached the place in the afternoon of the same day by the steamer 'Benares.' Just after his arrival, he was instructed by the Commissioner of Bhagalpur to "take a *bazar* with him," as, under the then circumstances, he would "find no *bazar* or provisions of any kind." The Collector of Bhagalpur was also asked to send provisions to Colgong "in a boat once a week." But later on that day, the Commissioner of Bhagalpur requested Major Shuckburgh to adopt such measures as he thought fit for the defence of Bhagalpur before proceeding to Colgong, "as intelligence had arrived from the interior on that day that the insurrection was spreading in the direction of Bhagalpur." Some villages, including Barkope, Dhurma, and Bhoorea (which was within 20 miles of Bhagalpur and lay direct on the road leading to it from the south-east), were plundered on the 18th of July, a large number of "frightened inhabitants" were "flocking in every hour (at Bhagalpur) with tales of fresh atrocities," and the panic was "consequently intense." Several Europeans, including the wife and sister-in-law of one of the road-inspectors, had been killed, and "the Railway operations entirely stopped."[100]

The Hill Rangers (Lt. Fagan Commanding at Bhagalpur, Sergeant Major 1, Native officers 3, Havi'dars 5, Naiks 10, Sepoys 119, Recruits 54), then stationed at Bhagalpur, were "engaged to guard the Treasury, Jail and *cutcheris*"[101] in the

99 Letter from the Commissioner of Bhagalpur to Major Burroughs, dated the 20th July, 1855. The Commissioner thanked Mr. Pepper for the help rendered by him and requested him to lend some elephants.

100 Letter from the Commissioner of Bhagalpur to Major-General Lloyd, Commanding at Dinapore, dated the 17th July, 1855, 10 P. M., para. 7.

101 Commissioner's letter to Major Shuckburgh, dated the 17th July, 1855, para. 3.

city. On the Commissioner's requisition, Major Shuckburgh "deemed it advisable to remain" at Bhagalpur "with the Head-quarters of his Regiment for the present," and to send to Major Burroughs 200 men under command of Lieut. Rubie on board the steamer 'Benares.' Major Burroughs was asked to send back his (the Commissoner's) portion of the Hill Rangers for the defence of Bhagalpur. Further, Major-General Lloyd of Dinapore was requested by the Commissioner through a letter. dated the 18th July, to send down more infantry as well as the Irregular Cavalry, for which he had been already written to him, and also a few Howitzers. The Commissioner also requested the Government of Bengal on the same day to "be pleased to send up more troops by steamer," as there was no certainty as to what extent the Santals might "devastate the district unless subdued promptly with a firm hand."[102] He considered that to be the most proper time "to strike the blow," for the *Damin-i-koh*, and the country to the south of Bhagalpur, were not then "particularly unhealthy," as they usually became after the rains.[103] The Magistrate and the Assistant Magistrate of Bhagalpur being absent from the station, and the Commissioner himself, finding it "utterly impossible to go singlehand,"[104] invested on his own responsibility Mr. R. N. Shore with magisterial powers.[105] He also wrote to Mr. F. Vincent, Deputy Magistrate of Barh,[106] on the 18th July, to come down to act as Deputy Magistrate of Bhagalpur to "aid him in quelling the rebellion," which had "assumed a very alarming aspect." The Commissioner and the Magistrate of Patna were requested by him to relieve Mr. Vincent of his office

102 Letter from the Commissioner of Bhagalpur to the Secretary to the Government of Bengal, dated the 18th July, 1855, 11 P. M., para. 3.

103 *Ibid.*

104 *Ibid.* (The Commissioner observed : "Since the outbreak commenced I have not had a night's rest for reports are coming in at all hours and require immediate attention.")

105 *Ibid.*

106 In some unpublished contemporary English records, preserved in the Record Room of the District Judge of Patna, Mr. Vincent is referred to as a highly capable officer.

at Barh, and the Magistrate of Monghyr was also asked to relieve him of the charge of the Monghyr *thannas* attached to the sub-division of Barh. The Judge of Bhagalpur was requested on the same date to "substitute Burkundazes for the guard of Hill Rangers on duty" in his office.

The Commissioner received from Calcutta an Electric Telegraph message (of the 15th July) on the 18th July, informing him that he must not depend on the troops from Berhampore for relieving Rajmahal, as the Government was of opinion that officers at Rajmahal should be appointed from Bhagalpur. He then wrote to the Bengal Government at 11 P.M., on the same day, that he thought of sending the steamer 'Meghna' with Captain Sherwill, and a small detachment of the Hill Rangers, on the next day, for the protection of the inhabitants there, and he recommended the appointment of an "active, intelligent and prudent Deputy Magistrate (not a Native) for Rajmahal."

The insurrection having by that time "assumed all the characteristics of a rebellion,"[107] the Commissioner "deemed it necessary for the protection of the lives and properties of the peaceable inhabitants of the district to proclaim martial law against the Santals."[108] The proclamation offered "large rewards for the apprehension of the Insurgent chiefs"[109]: for the "principal chief Rs. 10,000, for each of the Dewans (supposed to be about 3 or 4 in number) Rs. 5,000, and for each of the minor chiefs of Pergunnuhs Rs. 1,000."[110] But while it sanctioned "the destruction of the rebels found in arms," it carefully enjoined "*that their families be spared*," as "*the British Government does not make War against women and children*." The Commissioner informed Major Burroughs, on the 19th of July, that he should

[107] Letters, dated the 19th July, 1855, from the Commissioner of Bhagalpur, (1) to Major Burroughs, Camp Colgong, (2) to Mr. C. E. Chapman at Colgong, and (3) to Mr. Richardson, Magistrate of Bhagalpur then at Rajmahal.

[108] *Ibid.*

[109] Letter from the Commissioner of Bhagalpur to the Secretary to the Government of Bengal, dated the 18th July, 11 P.M.

[110] *Ibid.*

thereafter act on his own responsibility (that is, without the "presence of the civil power") in taking such measures as he considered fit for the "extirpation of the rebels,"[111] and that Mr. Chapman's duties in his camp were thenceforth to be confined to helping him "in obtaining information and furnishing supplies and carriages."[112] He also wrote to Mr. James Allan, Civil Assistant Surgeon of Bhagalpur, on the same date, to take proper care of the men sent to his hospital after being wounded by the Santal insurgents, even by supplying them with food at the expense of the Government.[113]

Disturbances in other Quarters—Godda, Pakur, Maheshpur, Murshidabad, and Birbhum

Disturbances had spread to other quarters with great rapidity. Mr. John Fitzpatrick, 'a very intelligent (indigo) farmer,' stationed at Godda, wrote to the Commissioner of Bhagalpur, on the 11th July, that a fearful panic had "seized the inhabitants of that neighbourhood since the perpetration of the barbarous murders on the 7th instant," and that six bands of Santals "to the amount (number) of several thousands—not under 20—are proceeding to the place where the pretended Soobah has set up his standard and they have threatened the Bengalees residing in those parts that they will return with an order from the Soobah for their extermination." Towards the Amber *paragana* (in the Zamindari of the Pakur Raj), one Singhrai Santal of Lakshanpur joined Gocho Manjhi. After having plundered the said village, they proceeded to Litipara, where there lived two rich *mahājans*, named Isree Bhakat and Tilak Bhakat, "whose ill-gotten wealth had made them immensely rich and who were the greatest eyesore of the Santals, whose heart-blood their sole business was to drink

111 The Commissioner's letter to Major Burroughs, dated the 10th July, 1855.

112 *Ibid.*

113 *Ibid*, dated the 20th July, 1855.

up.''.[114] Having already received information about the disturbances at Panchkeṭbia, these *mahājans* had fled away from their home, leaving a portion of their wealth in charge of their *gomasta*, Thootha Bhakat, who had "made himself notorious even amongst the Bhakats for his devising and exercising inhuman cruelties on the debtors of Isree and Tilak Bhakats.'' [115] The Santals plundered the shops of Isree and Tilak and killed the said *gomasta*. Some of the shopkeepers and *moiras* of the village Jitpur had concealed themselves within hollows of Mohul trees. But the Santals being informed of this through their *diku* (non-Santal) spies found them out and put them to death. Manik Sunri, and his son, of the village Karmghati, were killed with arrows by one Khela Santal. Thence the Santals proceeded to Hiranpur *bazar*. They plundered it and went away to Mansingpur, where they were joined by one Tirbhuban Santal *alias* Thakur of Fursadihi in Ambar *paragana*.[116] Being reinforced by a large number of low caste *dikus* (non-Santals), the Santal insurgents then proceeded to Sangrampur, about two miles to the north of Pakur, and plundered and burnt there the house of a rich Mussalman agriculturist named Rahamdi Mandal. This naturally excited panic in the minds of the inhabitants of Pakur Babu Jagabandhu Ray of Kanchantala, the then *diwan* of the Zamindar of Ambar *paragana*, consulted the villagers of Pakur as to how that place could be protected against the ravages of the Santal insurgents. He sent an elephant-driver named Rohsan Mahut to Jangipur to purchase " as much gunpowder as he could get and return with it to Pakur,'' and, in the meanwhile, ordered the sepoys and servants there to stock brick-bats, stones, etc., on the roof of the house of the local zamindar. The villagers were asked to keep their women and children within the compound of the zamindar's house till the rising was suppressed. But on Rohsan Mahut's returning to Pakur with only a small quantity

[114] Pakur Record [115] *Ibid* [116] *Ibid.*

of gunpowder, the *diwan* considered himself helpless and ordered the villagers to save their lives and property somehow or other. Thereupon, the panic became intense, as Mr. Chakravarty has described in the following language: " Then there arose loud wailings of the females, children shrieked and screamed, men talked nonsense and rushed hither and thither without any fixed aim ; fathers left aside their crying children unheeded ; no one cared for the old, the infirm, and the sickly. There was tying and untying of bundles, everything turned upside down and mixed up helter and skelter promiscuously. In short, a confused and heart-rending scene ensued which can be better imagined than described. We were at the time only six years of age, yet we remember vividly the scene of that hour of general woe and confusion and the impression left in our mind will never be obliterated. The fear and anxiety with which the terrible long night passed away beggar any description. But long before the day dawned almost the whole village became empty.........In this sad plight the villagers left their homes not knowing where to go, what food to give to the children when they would cry for hunger. All the eatables, all the money, utensils, furniture, in short, everything they possessed was left behind, their only aim and only object being to put as much distance as possible between the Santals and themselves." The runaway people wanted to cross over to the other side of the Ganges for safety, but the river was then in a high flood, which had reached even Ballabhpur, lying just to the east of Pakur. Boats were available with great difficulty, and Mr. Charles Maseyk, the indigo-planter of Kadamsair, rendered great help to the panic-stricken people by supplying them with boats.[117]

[117] A descendant of the first Maseyk (a Dutch trader who found his way overland to India *via* Aleppo, settled in Bengal in 1769-70, and married a local Muslim wife), who owned Indigo factories in Murshidabad and other places, inherited the purchased business and factories of Grant, of the East India Company in North Bengal, possessed Zamindaries in Santal Paraganas, and assisted the Government, in the suppression of the insurrection. His last descendant died at Purulia in October, 1934. Kadamsair is half a mile to the east of my native village Jhikarhati. Remains of the old indigo factory are to be found there even now.

. After having plundered Sangrampur, the Santal insurgents reached Pakur and kept the place almost in a state of siege for three days and nights. On the fourth day, *i.e.*, on the 12th of July, 1855, Sidhu, Kanhu, Chand and Bhairab entered the house of the local zamindar,[118] but they could not get wealth up to their expectation because most of it, including a precious jewel, with which the *rajahs* used to decorate their family god Madanmohan, had been shifted elsewhere. They then plundered the houses of many other villagers and robbed them of their wealth. One Brahmin named Radhanath Pande, a bed-ridden paralytic patient, and one Lakshman Mandal, who being a lame man could not run away, were brutally murdered. Two old women were, however, not only spared by them but also respectfully provided with some food and money. Rani Kshemasundari, the then zamindar of Pakur, had at first taken refuge at Jangipur with her family idol Madanmohan; but later on she came back to Jhikarhati, a large and prosperous village in her zamindari, where she remained for some time till peace was restored. "Although herself a great loser, she materially helped her subjects to rebuild their houses and to subsist till the next crops."

After the Santals had left Pakur, Dindayal Ray, the richest money-lender of that place, with his brother Nandakumar Ray and his followers, Sristidhar Poddar, Nilkamal Mandal, Nitai Mandal and Jadav Mandal, returned there. He was exceedingly glad to see that his treasures, hidden under the ground, were safe. He foolishly proclaimed that the zamindar of Pakur having left the place, he was thenceforth the zamindar of Ambar *paragana*. His party proceeded every day to the neighbouring Santal villages and committed various oppressions on the women and children of the Santals. But he soon received divine retribution for his rapacities. One day, he with his brother Nandakumar and his sister Bimala went for a bath to a tank called Chowdhuripukur, lying to the east of Pakur,

118 *Vide* Appendix B

when all of a sudden a large number of Santals appeared there. Nandakumar and Bimala fled away instantly and thus saved their lives, but Dindayal being a corpulent and old fellow could not leave the spot. The Santals fell upon him with bows, arrows, swords and *tangis* (axes), and set on him their ferocious dogs, who tore flesh from his limbs. Before the Santals dealt upon him the final blow, Jagannath Sirdar, who was formerly a servant of Dindayal Ray but had later joined the Santals, lopped off his limbs bit by bit with a *tangi*, exclaiming: "With those fingers you counted your interest and ill-begotten wealth! With this hand you snatched away food from the mouths of the hungry poor!" The Santals took Dindayal's head to the temple of Siva Chakrapaniswar, situated within a few yards from the scene of the tragedy, and placed it in a niche in the wall of the temple, which they painted with his blood.[118a] Dindayal's sister Bimala, who had concealed herself in a ditch lying close by, saw the tragic end of her brother, and from her the inhabitants of Pakur heard all the particulars regarding her brother's murder.

After leaving Pakur, the Santal insurgents proceeded to Ballabhpur, on the eastern border of Pakur, and killed there one Ghaneshyam Maria, a blacksmith by profession having a very strong constitution, two *bairagis* or professional mendicants, and two Mussalman *fakirs*, while they were cooking their food under a banian tree. They next plundered the villages Kalikapur, Ballabhpur, Baliharpur, Sahabazpur, and Nabinagar,[119] and advanced further east towards the border of the Murshidabad District. Mr. Toogood, Magistrate of Murshidabad, had left Berhampore for Aurangabad, on the 11th July, 1855, with a party of 400 men of 7th Regiment N. I. stationed there. On hearing of the advance of the Santals, he was detained at the indigo factory of Mr. H.

118a This temple remained in a dilapidated condition till a few years back, faint marks of blood being visible in the inner side of the walls even then.

119 I have noted the abovementioned facts from the work of Babu Digambar Chakravarty.

Maseyk at Dhulian, whence he sent a party of 160 *barkandazes* for the protection of the factory of Mr C. Maseyk (brother of the former) at Kadamsair.[120] After plundering the *kachari* of the zamindar of Ambar *paragana* (Pakur Raj) at Jhikarhati, the insurgents had raided the factory of Mr. C. Maseyk at Kadamsair, but the latter "with two other gentlemen, armed with fowling-pieces and stationed on a boat in the middle of a nullah, which commanded the approach to the premises, kept at bay the whole Santal army, wounded some, and captured one prisoner."[121] The 160 police *barkandazes*, who had been sent from Dhulian, "safely hid themselves in the high grass and seeds that lined the nullah's banks."

The Berhampore troops arrived at Kadamsair on the 13th July after the Santals had already moved from that place. They pursued the insurgents to Palsa on the 14th July, but the latter evaded capture and proceeded to Maheshpur. The house of the Rajah of Maheshpur was plundered and robbed of much wealth.[122] The troops of the 7th Regiment N. I. had an engagement, in the morning of the 15th July, with 3,000 or 4,000 Santals, who charged them "three times but were finally defeated."[123] Sidhu, Kanhu and Bhairab "were themselves shot, though not mortally, and 200 other Santals killed and wounded; above Rs. 7,000 in cash and Rs. 4,000 worth of goods, all plundered property, were recovered."[124] Two hundred men of 7th Regiment N. I. fell upon 5,000 of the insurgents near Pakur on the bank of the

120 Calcutta Review, 1856.

121 *Ibid.*

122 This is asserted by all the local records.

"Pouñchila Sāntāl save uccarave Maheśpur giye |
Luṭila dusṭācaya rājālaya dhanaratna nila |
Nila sava resamibasan svarnabhuṣan |
....
Panchkeṭbia Record.

123 Letter from the Commissioner of Bhagalpur to Major Lloyd at Dinapore, dated the 21st July, 1855.

124 Calcutta Review, 1856.

Tarai river,[125] and routed them completely, "killing great numbers and without single loss of life (on their own side)." [126] Two unfortunate English ladies, Mrs. Thomas and Miss Pell,[127] and three European gentlemen, Mr. Henshawe (Mr. Hennessy) [128] and his two sons, were murdered by a party of the insurgents under the guidance of Tirbhuban Santal, near Maharajpur.[129] Four blacksmiths, Lal Lohar and Prit Ram Lohar of Majurhati (later on of Kowadhab), Heera Lohar of Majurhati, and Motiram Lohar, who was for some time *chowkidar* of Patna (near Barharwa), Majurhati, and Beejpur, swore before the Special Commissioner for the suppression of the insurrection at Dumka to having seen Tirbhuban murder Mr. Henshawe.[130] They narrated that the insurgents first "assembled at Patna Bunglow under Tirbhuban and Mansing Manjhee (Manjhi) of Borio. Roopoo, Manjhee (*Manjhi*) of Majurhati and *Des Manjhee* [131] to Tumboo *Pergunaite* (*Parganait*) of Chota Kangela (Kānjola), was present with them and collected some *fouj* ; Meghoo, Manjhee (*Manjhi*) of Barmasia, also joined their party ; Ruchka, Roopoo's brother and *Chuckladar*, served as a guide ; and Singree, *Parganait* of Majurhati, was also one of the leaders. They all proceeded to Bhooepara where the Sahebs had assembled, near the 'Haut'; two Sahebs were on one elephant and one was on horseback ; being pursued by the Santals the Sahebs ran towards Maharajpur and they got as far as the *Jheel* (marshy land) east of Maharajpur when they were surrounded by the Santals who killed them with Furshas (axes). Mungut Santal, a ryot of Koachpara (formerly

125 Pakur Record.

126 Letter from the Commissioner of Bhagâlpur to Major Burroughs at Colgong, dated the 21st July, 1855.

127 Calcutta Review, 1856.

128 The old bungalow of Mr. Hennessy is still standing at Rajmahal.

129 From a document preserved in the Record Office of the D.C. of Dumka.

130 *Ibid.* Bijoo Santal, a ryot of Bhoraband, also gave evidence about Tirbhuban's murdering Mr. Henshawe.

131 As the *Manjhi* has an assistant in the village, so the *Parganait* has an assistant in his jurisdiction called the *Des-manjhi*.

of Kendwa), confessed having killed Mr. Henshawe's eldest son." It is stated by Babu Digambar Chakravarty that Sidhu and Kanhu did not support the murder of these European ladies and gentlemen. They even punished some of the culprits.

In Birbhum also, the insurrection had become formidable at Nalhati, Rampurhat, Nagore, Suri, Langulia, Gurjori, and other places. In fact, by the 20th of July, the revolt "had spread and was in activity" from Taldanga at the south-west of Birbhum, on the Grand Trunk Road, and Sainthia at the south-east, to Bhagalpur and Rajmahal on the Ganges at the north-west and north-east of the Bhagalpur district.[132] In order to prevent the advance of the Santals to the south of the Damodar river and of the Grand Trunk Road, and also to protect the adjacent territories, the Ramgurh Irregular Light Horse, the Governor-General's Bodyguard, the 37th Regiment, and 200 Nizamat sepoys from the Guard of the Nawab of Murshidabad with 30 of his elephants besides 32 horse, and subsequently the 63rd Regiment N. I., had been put in motion.[133] As we have already seen, the 7th and the 31st Regiment N. I. had been employed on the Murshidabad border; and the Hill Rangers, and portions of the 10th, the 42nd, and the 13th Regiment N. I., coming from Dinapore, had been engaged towards Bhagalpur and Colgong. Garrison posts of the 7th and 31st Regiments N. I., and the Nizamat troops, were kept at Pakur, Phudkipur, and some neighbouring places, "protecting the country on either side of the Murshidabad border from the Birbhum boundary to the Ganges river."[134]

132 Calcutta Review, 1856

133 *Ibid.*

134 *Ibid.*

CHAPTER III

SUPPRESSION OF THE INSURRECTION

Anxiety of the Bhagalpur Commissioner

The Commissioner of Bhagalpur thought that "simultaneous movements on the insurgents by Bhagalpur, Birbhum and Rajmahal troops may be of great effect."[135] So he wrote to Major Burroughs at Colgong, on the 20th July, strongly urging him "to adopt offensive measures against the Rebels."[136] But being anxious for the safety and defence of Bhagalpur, he changed his plan on the next day, and accordingly informed Major Burroughs that he should return to Bhagalpur with the 100 men of the Hill Rangers, and that Major Shuckburgh should proceed to Colgong with the 200 men of the 40th Regiment leaving 100 of them behind at Bhagalpur.[137] He wrote to Mr. W. T. Tucker, Magistrate of Monghyr, on the same day, cordially approving of his plan of "entertaining a guard of one thousand Ghatwals[138] at a monthly charge of Three Thousand and Fifty Rupees to watch the passes" of his district, but at the same time requested him to be very "careful to ascertain their loyalty" before engaging their services, for they, being of a "cognate tribe with the Santals," might "prove treacherous in hour of need." At Rajmahal, Mr. Richardson had with him

135 The Commissioner's letter to Major Burroughs, dated the 19th July, 1855.

136 *Ibid*, dated the 20th July, 1855.

137 *Ibid*, dated the 21st July, 1855.

138 The *Ghatwals* were hill-chiefs, who raised small levies for the defence of the *ghats* or passes through the hills ; they were granted in return tenures of land called *Ghatwale* tenures.—*Santal Paraganas District Gazetteer*, p 219 ; *Monghyr District Gazettier*, p. 165.

only. 120 men of the 7th Regiment N. I., and 38 men of the Hill Rangers, which he considered "utterly insufficient," and so sent to the Commissioner of Bhagalpur "an urgent requisition for more troops."[139] The latter, therefore, wrote to Major-General Lloyd at Dinapore, on the 21st July, that more troops were "necessary for suppresing the rebellion......which has assumed such a very alarming aspect. Not a day passes without fresh atrocities being perpetrated, villages plundered and burnt and the unfortunate inhabitants massacred without respect to age or sex."[140] Mr. Charles Harrington Barnes, indigo-planter of the Colgong, Pirpainti, and Pyalapore concerns, who had lived in the district (of Bhagalpur) for more than fifteen years, offered his "services to render all necessary aid to the Troops proceeding against the Santal rebels." He was, therefore, given "unrestricted powers" by the Commissioner of Bhagalpur "to obtain what may be necessary for the exigencies of public service and to call on all Police officers, Zamindars, and others for their assistance."[141] Mr. Chapman, then stationed with the troops at Colgong, was asked to return to Bhagalpur, where his services were more urgently required.

Captain Sherwill proceeded on board the 'Meghna' from Bhagalpur at noon of the 19th July, with 40 men of the Hill Rangers, to help Mr. Richardson at Rajmahal. He reached there on the 20th July at 9-30 A.M., but finding that Lieutenant Lockart of the 7th Regiment N. I. had already come there, and that his help was not, therefore, required, he left that place at noon, and reached Colgong on Saturday the 21st July at 9-30 A.M., with a view to joining Major Burroughs' troops. But as Major Burroughs' party then "amounted to considerably more than 400 Rank and File, *viz.*, 200 of the

139 Letter from the Commissioner to Major-General Lloyd at Dinapore, dated the 21st July, 1855.

140 Commissioner's letter to Major General Lloyd, dated 21st July, 1855.

141 Letter from the Commissioner to Mr. Charles Harrington Barnes at Colgong, dated the 21st July, 1855.

40th Regiment and 240 of the Hill Rangers," [142] he left Colgong at 1-30 P.M. on the 21st July, and reached Bhagalpur at 4-30 P.M. with 16 prisoners from Rajmahal, and also 18 prisoners from Colgong, who had been arrested, "armed with bows and poisoned arrows looting near Colgong," in the morning of 21st July, by the *jagirdars* of Mysumoonder, lying 2 miles S.E. of Colgong.[143] Of these 18 prisoners, 8 were ***hillmen*** and 5 ***benias,*** which showed that "armed bands of Hillmen, Bonyahs (*benias*) and other low castes" were "pillaging as well as Santals around Colgong." [144] Captain Sherwill noted the following in his Memo., regarding his voyage to, and from, Rajmahal: "The Santals are in force all along the high road from Peellapoor (Pyalapore) to Rajmahal having been joined by the hillmen in some places. Villages all round Colgong have been told off for loot and burning by the Santals and their arrangements have been carried on for the last four days in the view of Colgong. Numerous Zemindars have come into Colgong begging that the Troops may be allowed to move out but they have not (done so) up to noon of 21st July. Hourly notices are brought in of villages being looted and the people about to be murdered but the military have not moved out. Major Burroughs says he will move out this afternoon (21st July) to try and endeavour to stop the burnning. The villages on fire seem to the East and South-east—and are visib'e more as I wrote. The Sepoys of the 40th Regiment N. I. are most anxious to march off against the insurgents." [145]

Inactivity of Major Burroughs' Troops at Colgong: Plans of the Bhagalpur Commissioner

Inspite of all precautions, very little had been done by Major Burroughs at Colgong, Pirpainti, and Narainpur till

[142] Letter from the Commissioner of Bhagalpur to the Secretary to the Government of Bengal, dated the 21st July, 1855. 11 P.M.

[143] *Ibid.* [144] *Ibid* [145] *Ibid.*

the 26th July to suppress the insurrection.[146] All direct communications between Bhagalpur and Rajmahal being suspended, Mr. George, the Inspecting Postmaster, endeavoured to reopen these by organising an establishment of fast-pulling boats.[147] The Commissioner of Bhagalpur deeply regretted that "the troops have been allowed to remain inactive," [148] and solicited the permission of the Government of Bengal to issue another Proclamation like that of the 18th July. He actually issuod a Proclamation on the 23rd July declaring therein that "other castes of persons besides Santals who may take up arms against the peaceable subjects to Government are to be considered rebels in like manner and treated accordingly," [148a] and circulated it on the 25th July, 1855, to the Judges of Bhagalpur, Purneah, Tirhut, Murshidabad, the Collectors of Bhagalpur, Monghyr, Purneah, the Magistrates of Patna, Murshidabad, Bhagalpur, Monghyr, Purneah, Tirhut, and to the Moulavi in charge of the Magistrate's office at Bhagalpur. Lala Sheo Sahay was appointed a *surbarakar* (*sarbarāhakāra*, supplier) by the Commissioner of Bhagalpur to procure provisions, and Mr. J. Dacosta, Munsiff of Bhagalpur, consented to take charge of the carriage department. Both of them rendered much help to the Collector of Bhagalpur.[149] Mr. J. W. Money of the Civil Service at Monghyr also volunteered his services in place of Mr. Chapman,[150] who, on his return to Bhagalpur, had to officiate as the Joint Magistrate with full powers till the Magistrate could return there. Mr R. N. Shore was appointed the Commissioner's assistant. Mr. Vincent,

146 *Ibid.*

147 Letter from the Commissioner of Bhagalpur to the Secretary to the Government of Bengal, dated the 26th July, 1855.

148 Letter from the Commissioner of Bhagalpur to the Secretary to the Government of Bengal, dated the 21st July, 1855, 11 P.M., para. 6.

148a Letters Nos. 430 and 431 in the Commissioner's Record office at Bhagalpur.

149 Letter from the Commissioner of Bhagalpur to the Collector of Bhagalpur, dated the 23rd July, 1855.

150 Letter from the Commissioner of Bhagalpur to the Collector of Monghyr, dated the 24th July, 1855

Deputy Magistrate of Barh, had been asked, as we have already noted, to assist the Commissioner of Bhagalpur, but the Commissioner of Patna objected to his leaving Barh.[151] Major Burroughs was ordered by the Commissioner, on the evening of the 26th July, that " a strong detachment (of about 200 or 300 men) be immediately sent to Rajmahal,—and a similar one to the south-west of Bhagalpur near Barkope and Godda besides other detachments in other directions."

But the Commissioner of Bhagalpur soon received an Electric Telegraph message from Calcutta informing him that his Proclamations of the 18th and the 23rd July were illegal and " must be recalled and cancelled and each reward offered therein reduced one-half." [152] He obeyed the orders instantly, and wrote accordingly on the 26th July to the Magistrates and Judges of different places (as already noted), and also to Mr. Pontet, Superintendent of the *Damin-i-koh*.[153] But he still advocated " Extreme Measures " for " Extreme Cases " and waited for " further instructions of the Lieutenant-Governor on the subject." [154]

Captain Waterman came from Dinapore to Bhagalpur at 8 A.M. of the 25th July, with 300 men of the 13th Regiment N. I.[155] The panic at Bhagalpur abated after his arrival, and the Commissioner no longer apprehended any attack on that city.[156] He expected that a " comparatively small force will be quite sufficient for the defence of the place in any extremity notwithstanding its great extent (more than five miles long) provided it could be handled by an energetic officer." [157] He also hoped to send a " strong detachment " to Rajmahal after the rest of the 13th Regiment N. I. had come from Dinapore.[158] Inspite of " great exertions " being made to procure

151 Letter from the Commissioner of Bhagalpur to the Secretary to the Government of Bengal, dated the 26th July, 1855.

152 *Ibid.* 153 *Ibid.* 154 *Ibid.*

155 Letter from the Commissioner to Major Burroughs, dated the 26th July, 1885,

156 *Ibid*, para. 6. 157 *Ibid.* 158 *Ibid*, para. 5.

elephants, only 38 could be obtained by the 26th July and 12 more were then expected.[159] The Zamindars had "shown the utmost readiness in furnishing supplies," which was "a proof not only of their goodwill towards the Government but their extreme anxiety to aid the troops employed in suppressing the insurrection."[160] Mr. W. T. Tucker, Magistrate of Monghyr, was also "exerting himself most energetically to inspire the people with confidence and in adopting measures for preserving the peace and preventing the insurrection spreading towards the west."[161] In order to accommodate the additional troops expected from Dinapore, the Commissioner wrote to the Secretary to the Local Committee of Public Instruction at Bhagalpur, on the 28th July, 1855, to obtain the sanction of the Local Committee of Public Instruction to "appropriate the Government school-house for that purpose" by paying rent for the whole or part, as occupied.

March of Major Shuckburgh and Captain Francis

In the meanwhile, Major Shuckburgh, along with Captain Sherwill and 300 men of the 40th Regiment N. I., had proceeded from Bhagalpur on the 25th July, with a view "to take up a line of his own going south to Dighee and thence to the east, till he reaches the Damin-i-koh, when he can either proceed northwards to Telleagurhee (Teliagarhi) and join Major Burroughs or to the south with the view of entering the Hills by the new dawk road leading to Rajmahal."[162] He rached Dighee (12 miles south of Colgong) on the 26th, proceeded on the 27th to Dukyto (Dakatia) and Lorundree (Lohundea, half-way between

159 *Ibid*, para 12

160 *Ibid*.

161 *Ibid*, para. 13.

162 Letter from the Commissioner of Bhagalpur to the Secretary to the Government of of Bengal, dated the 26th July, 1855

Dighee and Borio); both the places lying about 12 miles beyond Dighee in E.S.E. direction, and expected to reach Borio on the following day.[163] Referring to the advance of Major Shuckburgh, the Commissioner of Bhagalpur sent, on the 28th July, 1855, the following instructions to Major Burroughs, who had remained till then at Pyalapore with 200 men of the 40th Regiment N. I.: "If you were only to push your party in the same vigorous and determined manner towards Bhuggya (three miles to the west of Mirzachowki Railway station), the rebels would be hemmed in between the two forces and a most decisive blow might be struck.........." Mr. Barnes, the indigo-planter, whom the Commissioner had directed to relieve Major Burroughs, had to accompany Major Shuckburgh, and so another arrangement being necessary, the Faujdari Nazir of Bhagalpur, Shaikh Azid Bux, was deputed by him to Major Burroughs' camp to "represent the civil power on all requisite occasions" till he could send there an "officer of a superior grade to supply his place." Captain Francis with 200 men of the 13th Regiment, N. I. accompanied by Mr. W. J. Money [164] as civil authority, marched in the morning of the 28th of July towards Amarpur and Bowsee (Baunsi, Mandar Hills), south of Bhagalpur, to quell the insurrection, which was very "ripe in that quarter." The Deputy Magistrate of Deoghur, alarmed by the advance of the Santals, had by that time taken to flight.[165]

Additional Troops from Dinapore

Lieutenant-Colonel Liptrap, with 250 rank and file of the 42nd Regiment N. I., reached Bhagalpur by steamer in the morning of the 29th July, and the remainder of the 13th Regiment N. I. (about

[163] Letter from the Commissioner of Bhagalpur to the Officer Commanding Head Quarters of the 13th Regiment N. I. (then expected at Bhagalpur), dated the 28th July, 1855.

[164] Letter from the Commissioner of Bhagalpur to the Secretary to the Government of Bengal, dated the 18th July, 1855, 10 P.M., para. 6.

[165] *Ibid.*

350 men) also came there in the afternoon of that day under the command of Major Bruere.[166] On their arrival, the Commissioner immediately arranged with Lt.-Col. Liptrap that 250 rank and file of the 13th Regiment N. I. should proceed to Rajmahal on board the steamer 'Lady Hackwell,' and that he should "take command of the troops in this (Bhagalpur) district (towards Colgong)." Major Burroughs was to return to Bhagalpur with the Hill Rangers, whose place would be occupied "by the troops of the line," and "then a vigorous effort will doubtless be made by the Detachments at Pyalapoor (Pyalapore) and Dighee to co-operate with those at Rajmahal and elsewhere."[167] Being unacquainted with the peculiar circumstances under which Mr. Richardson had then been placed at Rajmahal, the Commissioner could not give him "definite instructions regarding the direction in which the troops would proceed" after joining him—whether towards Sakrigali, or towards Pakur, or into the heart of the *Damin*.[168]

Attempt of the Commissioner of Bhagalpur to collect Elephants

The Commissioner of Bhagalpur was making "every effort to obtain more elephants."[169] On the 30th July, he wrote to the Magistrates of Tirhut, Purneah, Monghyr, and the Deputy Magistrates of Kishanganj and Madhipura, to send all the elephants they could collect. He observed in his letters to them that in sending the elephants they should "furnish a list of them with their names, the names of their owners and *mahuts* (elephant-drivers), and estimated value of

166 *Ibid*, dated the 29th July, 1855.

167 Letter from the Commissioner to Mr. Richardson, Magistrate of Bhagalpur at Rajmahal, dated the 29th July, 1855.

168 *Ibid*

169 *Ibid*.

each elephant.[170] "Government will pay a rupee a day for their use and guarantee compensation in the event of loss or injury." Fifty *Havildars* from Purneah joined Major Burroughs at Colgong, but he did not take any notice of the offer of elephants made by Mr. G. A. Pepper, Magistrate of Purneah, who thereupon left that place.[171]

Lloyd at Bhagalpur and Rajmahal

By the end of July, Major-General Lloyd arrived at Bhagalpur and took upon himself the "disposition of the Troops." [172] While given absolute powers over the movements of the military, Major-General Lloyd remained subject to the authority of the Civil power for non-military affairs. "It was not intended," wrote the Secretary to the Government of Bengal to the Commissioner of the Burdwan Division, on the 30th July, 1855, "that the military should act independently of the civil power against our own subjects ; but that the nature of the military operations necessary for dispersing and capturing the insurgents, and for putting down the rebellion, should be entirely in the hands of the military commanders." Major-General Lloyd left Bhagalpur for Rajmahal in the morning of the 2nd August, 1855,[173] and came back there on the 11th of August, 1855.[174]

170 Such a list is appended to a volume (preserved in the Record Office of the Commissioner of Bhagalpur), dealing with the letters of the Special Commissioner for the suppression of the Santal insurrection

171 Letters from the Commissioner of Bhagalpur to Major Burroughs and to the Magistrate of Purneah, dated the 30th July, 1855

172 Letter from the Commissioner of Bhagalpur to the Secretary to the Government of Bengal, dated the 31st July, 1855. The following arrangements were made for accommodating the troops at Bhagalpur : The Native Infantry were pitched in the compound of the cutchery of the Commissioner, who had also given up two out of the three rooms of the building "to shelter the officers from the inclemency of the weather."--Letter from the Commissioner of Bhagalpur to the Secretary to the Government of Bengal, dated the 11th August, 1855, para. 5. "The Government School-House was given up for the accommodation of the General and the artillery,—the General and his staff occupying one part of it and the artillery the other ; half of the school boys had been removed to an old mosque and the remainder to the Headmaster's own Bungalow "—*Ibid.*

173 *Ibid*, dated the 6th August, 1855

174 *Ibid*, dated the 11th August, 1855, para. 2.

Combined Efforts of the Military and the Civil Officers, the Zamindars, and the Indigo-Planters : Return of Comparative Security in the Damin-i-koh and the Plains

Since the end of July, the military officers adopted strong measures in different directions. Major Shuckburgh made "another successful raid against the Santals and destroyed a good deal of property, but as the insurgents fled at the approach of the Troops, instead of standing their grounds, he could not (in the absence of cavalry) get near enough to attack these persons with any effect."[175] Major Burroughs at last pushed on with his party towards Pyalapore and attacked some of the Santal villages.[176] Early in the morning of the 29th July, Captain Sherwill, and 150 sepoys of the 40th Regiment N. I. under command of Lieutenant Cahil, made 'a very successful' tour (in a N. E. direction from the camp at Dighee), during which they destroyed 12 Santal villages, 'full of plunders.' At Balbadda they saw the indigo factory, "which had been burnt by the Santals, still smouldering." At Chora, the Santals were "armed and apparently ready for action," but they fled into the jungles at the approach of the troops so that "very few of the insurgents were gone wounded"[177] The troops, however, "succeeded in securing a large supply of grain for the use of the Troops and the poor starving villagers who accompanied them and in capturing a great quantity of loot (plundered property) chiefly in the shape of brass vessels and upwards a thousand head of cattle besides goats and sheep." They also caught hold of one Ganapat Gawala, who was the "head spy and guide of the Santals in those parts and destroyed his residence consisting of 8 houses full of loot (plundered articles) ; among other things English chairs, a saddle, a lady's looking glass, besides immense quantities of grain and good native cloths."[178] Though the tour lasted for 9

175 *Ibid*, dated the 31st July, para. 2.

176 *Ibid*, para. 3.

177 *Ibid*, dated the 3rd August, 1855.

178 *Ibid*.

hours over 19 miles, 16 of which lay through wet paddy-fields, yet the troops "went on most cheerfully."[179] Thus, Captain Sherwill's "able assistance" was of great help to Major Shuckburgh's party, but he was soon summoned by Major-General Lloyd to join his staff at Rajmahal.[180] Major Shuckburgh's party moved on from Dighee to Bissohura (4 miles eastward) on the 1st August. After having properly arranged his camp, he sent Lieutenant Burn with 50 men to destroy a Santal village in the neighbourhood.[181] Scarcely had Lieutenant Burn marched for half an hour when he was attacked by about 600 Santals, "who were however routed being dead on the ground." Major Shuckburgh then started on the 2nd August in a south-eastern direction to Deadeh, and then north-east, through Khonerah and round the hills, to Lohundea "destroying 15 Santal villages by the way and clearing that part of the country of the rebels."[182] He wrote earnestly for more elephants without which, as he said, he could "scarcely move."[183]

As for Major Burroughs, he left Pyalapore on the 29th July, 1855, for Bhuggya (6½ miles S.E. of Pyalapore) and marched with no opposition from the insurgents, even "when small parties of 75 and 100 were sent against them."[184] He was without any civil authority with him, because the *Faujdari Nazir*, who had been selected for that position, could not reach Pyalapore before his departure from that place.[185] In the afternoon of the 29th July, Major Burroughs sent a detachment of 75 rank and file under Lieutenant Gordon to destroy the Santal villages of Munhan and Munkatro, situated to the west of his position, and in the morning of the following day he deputed Lieutenant Rubie with 100

[179] *Ibid.* [180] *Ibid*, para. 3.

[181] Letter from the Commissioner of Bhagalpur to Major General Lloyd at Rajmahal, dated the 6th August, 1855, para. 4.

[182] *Ibid.* [183] *Ibid.*

[184] Letter from the Commissioner of Bhagalpur to the Secretary to the Government of Bengal, dated the 3rd August, 1855, para. 4.

[185] *Ibid.*

men; "who made a detour to the North-west and destroyed the villages of Bugayah (Bhuggya), Titereah, Buskudar, Rangokitta, Hurrialiah, Kamuldeh and Bochai." [186] But Major Burroughs was soon relieved by Captain Waterman and left for Bhagalpur on the 6th of August.[187]

In the meanwhile, the detachment accompanying the Magistrate of Murshidabad had pursued the insurgents into the Hills, inflicted a defeat on Chand and Kanhu at Raghunathpur (on the Barharwa-Barhait road), and "burnt Bhugnadee and taken possession of Barhait, the stronghold of the insurgents," [188] on the 24th July.[189] A party of the Santals still hovered about the Luchmipore and Dhuldulee (Daldali) hills, situated near by, but the main body of the insurgents proceeded to the south-west of the district of Santal Paraganas towards Pusoye and Nonihat (on the Dumka-Godda road), and the movement extended still further westward.[190] The Commissioner of Bhagalpur, therefore, thought it advisable to send more troops towards the south and the south-west of Bhagalpur [191] in support of the detachment under Captain Francis, [192] who could not move from Baunsi on the 30th and the 31st July, because of heavy rains, "which completely saturated everything."[193] At 4 P.M. on the 1st August, Captain Francis' party reached the vicinity of Chooma Kotoe (Chunakuthi). It was about sunset when they fell upon the rebels, "who advanced boldly to the attack, sounding drums and performing extravagant gestures." [194] Captain Francis opened fire and wounded about 10 of them; on his side only two men were slightly wounded. Due to the approach of night, and his ignorance of the exact position

186 Letter from the Commissioner of Bhagalpur to Major-General Lloyd at Rajmahal, dated the 6th August, 1855, para. 4.

187 *Ibid.*

188 Letter from the Commissioner of Bhagalpur to the Secretary to the Government of Bengal, dated the 3rd August, 1855, para 5.

189 *Ibid.* 190 *Ibid.* 191 *Ibid.* 192 *Ibid.*

193 Letter from the Commissioner of Bhagalpur to Major-General Lloyd at Rajmahal, dated the 6th August, 1855, para. 5.

194 *Ibid.*

of Chunakuthi, Captain Francis thought it advisable to return to his camp.[195] Early in the morning of the 2nd August, the attack was renewed, but the rebels beat a retreat, and when Captain Francis reached Chunakuthi at about 7 A.M., he "found it evacuated but full of plunders of all descriptions."[196] Having burnt that place, his party proceeded to Barkope. Captain Francis had left a portion of his gunpowder and his heavy baggage at Baunsi under the charge of a guard of 40 men. The insurgents fell upon them on the 3rd August, but were repulsed "with the loss of seven of their number killed."[197] Mr. W. J. Money had come down from Monghyr and joined Captain Francis.[198] A detachment of 194 rank and file of the 42nd Regiment N. I., with a complement of Indian commissioned and non-commissioned officers and two European officers, also marched from Bhagalpur in the morning of the 11th August to reinforce Captain Francis, who was then expected "to co-operate with Major Shuckburgh in the contemplated attack on the Santals but in an opposite direction."[199]

The Santal insurgents ravaged the Birbhum district throughout the month of July. By the 20th of July, Mithijanpur and Narainpur were plundered by them[200]; and the Zamindar of the latter place rewarded Ghulam Ali Khan, the *daroga* of *thana* Afzalpur, with a sword and a piece of shawl for having gallantly defended his pucca house.[201] On the 21st of July, a party of the insurgents was opposed at Katmah by the Sardar Ghatwal of Kajoorea, a few other Ghatwals, and some Bengalees,[202] but by the 23rd "the large town of Gunpore," and many other villages, were destroyed by them.[203] They then plundered Nagore,

[195] *Ibid.* [196] *Ibid.* [197] *Ibid.*

[198] Letter from the Commissioner of Bhagalpur to the Secretary to the Government of Bengal, dated the 6th August, 1855.

[199] Letter from the Commissioner of Bhagalpur to the Secretary to the Government of Bengal, dated the 11th August, 1855, para. 6.

[200] Calcutta Review, 1856.

[201] *Ibid.* [202] *Ibid.* [203] *Ibid.*

situated 15 miles west of Suri, the Headquarters of the Birbhum district. Lieutenant Taulmain was killed " in an unadvised attack upon a superior force posted on the opposite side of a nullah," [204] but Lieutenant Dealamaine of the 56th Regiment N. I. was successful against the insurgents at Nungolea (*i.e* , Langulia).[205] Being then driven from Afzalpur, Nagore, and Mohuncha Hill (then a Trigonometrical Survey station), the insurgents proceeded to Kumrabad.[206] By the first week of August, they " in a great measure abandoned active opposition to the troops sent against them " [207]

The troops engaged against the insurgents were sometimes supplied with funds by the European indigo-planters. [208] Many of the Zamindars in the Bhagalpur and neighbouring districts lent elephants for service with the different detachments posted over the affected area. They also expressed their willingness " to receive no hire " but preferred to " lend them to the Government, only desiring that they should be well fed and taken care of during the period of their employment." [209] His Highness the Nawab Nazim of Murshidabad, too, lent a train of elephants at his personal expense. [210] Thus, energetic and combined efforts from different quarters—the Government troops, the Zamindars, and the planters—restored comparative security in the *Damin-i-koh* and the neighbouring plains by the beginning of the second week of August. So the Commissioner of Bhagalpur requested the Inspecting Postmaster General at Bhagalpur on the 8th August to reopen communications through the old line *via* Pyalapore, Tehagarhi, Sakrigali, and the new one *via* Borio. He

204 *Ibid.* 205 *Ibid.*

206 In the Dumka subdivision of the district of Santal Parganas

207 Letter from the Magistrate of Birbhum to the Special Commissioner, dated the 6th August, 1855.

208 Letter from the Commissioner of Burdwan to the officiating Collector of Birbhum, dated the 27th September, 1855, para. 2.

209 Letter from the Special Commissioner for suppressing the Santal insurrection to Captain R. D Macdonald, dated Berhampore, the 21st August, 1855.

210 *Ibid*, para. 7.

wrote to the Secretary to the Government of Bengal on the 11th August: " The communication is now open by that route (Borio route) to Rajmahal (and of course to Calcutta) and measures are being adopted for establishing the *Dawk Moonshees* and runners along that line, though confidence is not yet perfectly restored and the means of subsistence and shelter at the different stages have to be provided ; a delay of a few days may take place before the arrangements are completed."

Many Santals Still in Arms

But the insurrection was not yet completely suppressed. The " numbers (of Santal insurgents) in open arms (in certain parts) were still estimated to exceed 30,000 men."[211] Many of them were also proceeding towards Monghyr " into the village of Mulheapoor with the intention either of settling there, or of inciting the Santals of the country to rebellion."[212] The Commissioner of Bhagalpur, therefore, wrote, on the 11th of August, to Mr. W. T. Tucker, Magistrate of Monghyr: " .... they have as yet shown no signs of submission to Government ; but are on the contrary openly at war with our troops in this district and in those of Murshidabad and Birbhum; I, therefore, recommend your using every means in your power to prevent their entry within your jurisdiction. There is only one condition on which you can hold out to them any hope of conciliation and that is by their delivering up the chiefs of the present insurrection."

Strained Relations between the Bengal Government and the Commissioner of Bhagalpur

Since the close of July, the relations between the Bengal Government and Mr. Brown, the Commissioner of Bhagalpur, grew rather strained. The former accused the latter of " having

211 Calcutta Review, 1856.

212 Letter from the Commissioner of Bhagalpur to Mr. W. T Tucker, Magistrate of Monghyr, dated the 11th August, 1855.

failed to adopt offensive operations equally vigorous and effective as those which have been so effectively carried out" in the Murshidabad district,[213] and did not approve of his plan of offering high rewards for capturing the leaders of the insurrection. Mr. Brown thus defended his own conduct: "In fixing the amount of the rewards so large I had regard not only to the enormity of the offence and to the fearful loss of life and property which the insurrection was occasioning but also to the numerous loss of revenue and the immense cost to which Government would be put in the march of troops, etc., and I calculate that the apprehension of the chiefs would in comparison be cheaply purchased for the sums I named or even double."[214] Since the outbreak of the insurrection, a large number of non-Santals, such as *gowālās* (milkmen), *telis* (oilmen), *lohārs* (blacksmiths), and *bhunyās* (bhuiyas), besides many Santals, had been sent to Bhagalpur by the Police, who "found them with arms in their hands and unlawfully assembling for the purpose of committing riot or pillage."[215] The Commissioner of Bhagalpur thought that those people should be tried quickly by the officer in charge of the Magistrate's office instead of being detained for "any considerable length of time in Hajat,"[216] but he entertained "grave doubts" as to whether they could be tried "with advertence to the provisions of the Act V of 1811."[217] In his opinion, the provisions of that Act applied only to "Treason, Rebellion and other crimes against the state,"[218] and these could not be put into force till the Government had appointed a Commission for that purpose. But he regarded the cases alluded to as "simple attempts to commit riot and plunder,"[219] which might be disposed of by the Magistrate under "ordinary Regulation."[220] On the 2nd August, 1855, he solicited the

213 Letter from the Commissioner of Bhagalpur to the Secretary to the Government of Bengal, dated the 31st July, 1855.

214 *Ibid*, para. 4.

215 Letter from the Commissioner of Bhagalpur to the Judge of Bhagalpur, dated the 21st July, 1855.

216 *Ibid*, para. 2. 217 *Ibid*. 218 *Ibid*. 219 *Ibid*. 220 *Ibid*.

opinion of the Judge of Bhagalpur in this matter, but the latter did not approve of the Magistrate's disposing of any of those cases. On the 6th of August, he wrote to the Secretary to the Government of Bengal seeking his permission to appoint a sufficient number of civil officers (owing to their lack) "to act in a civil capacity with each Detachment in the field." He also requested the Government for early orders regarding the trial of persons "who had been seized and sent in charged with being concerned in the present insurrection."

Appointment of a Special Commissioner for the Suppression of the Insurrection

But the Commissioner's requests were not complied with by the Lieutenant-Governor, Mr. (afterwards Sir) Frederick James Halliday, who had formed an unfavourable opinion about his conduct in connection with the insurrection.[221] Mr. A. C. Bidwell, Commissioner of the Nadia Division, was appointed a 'Special Commissioner' to conduct, under the orders of the Bengal Government, "the measures necessary for the entire suppression of the insurection which has broken out among the Santal population and for restoring tranquillity to the disturbed districts."[222] He was requested by Mr. W. Grey, Secretary to the Government of Bengal, on the 6th August, 1855, to proceed quickly to Rajmahal and place himself in communication with Major-General Lloyd. He received the following instructions from him for his guidance: "3rd. The Lieutenant-Governor requests that you will report your proceedings as well as military measures that may be taken as frequently as possible. 4th. A few days since the Government received from the Magistrate of Bhagalpur a copy of a document which had been forwarded to that officer by the

[221] Letter from the Commissioner of Bhagalpur to the Secretary to the Government of Bengal, dated the 10th August, 1855.

[222] Letter from the Secretary to the Government of Bengal to Mr. A. C. Bidwell, dated the 6th August, 1855, para. 1.

Santals. A translation of this document is enclosed and the Lieutenant-Governor considers that, having regard to the tenor of it, and also to the circumstances that the Santals would appear, more particularly from the accounts received from the Birbhum District, already in a great measure to have abandoned active opposition to the troops sent against them, you should now take every means of publishing and proclaiming among them by written note both in the Hindi and Bengalee languages that the Government will freely pardon all who may tender a speedy submission, except those who shall be proved to have been the principal instigators and leaders of the insurrection, and those who shall be proved to have been principally concerned in the perpetration of any murder. They would be warned at the same time that against all who continue to offer resistance, prompt and severe measures will be unhesitatingly adopted, while, on the other hand, that as soon as complete submission is shown to the authority of Government, you will be prepared to receive and carefully enquire into all well-grounded complaints which they may have to prefer.

"5th. The Lieutenant-Governor has observed in several of the reports, public and private, that have come before him since the troops have been in the field. mention of Santal villages having been burnt in the course of active measures against the rebels. 6th. This may sometimes have happened unavoidably and sometimes he has no doubt, as in the case of Bhugnadihee, the chief position of the leading Santals near Burhait (Barhait), of the destruction of which he entirely approves, may have been done purposely with a view of striking terror and inflicting a summary and immediate punishment on leading rebels through their property in a particular and important instance likely to make a striking impression on all the subordinate insurgents.

"7th. But it is necessary to bear in mind that the Laws have not been suspended, and that a responsibility will attach to all acts of wanton and unnecessary severity, and even were it otherwise, it can never, the Lieutenant-

Governor believes, conduce to the early settlement of the present unhappy disturbances to make large bodies of armed men, our subjects, homeless and desperate. A few severe examples must be necessary and ought assuredly to be made but you will not let, the Lt.-Governor feels sure, overstep the bounds of that *true moderation and humanity which should distinguish all our dealings with our subjects, even the most perverse and misguided.*" [223]

The Hon'ble Mr. (afterwards Sir) Ashley Eden was appointed Mr. A. C Bidwell's first assistant with the powers of a Joint Magistrate and Deputy Collector, and Mr. Barnes, another assistant, with the powers of a Deputy Magistrate and Deputy Collector. Mr. Pontet was asked to consider himself as being under Mr. Bidwell's immediate orders during his special appointment in connection with the insurrection in the *Damin-i-koh*.

The Proclamation of the 17th August

Acting according to the instructions of the Bengal Government, the Special Commissioner issued, on the 17th August, a proclamation offering pardon to all except the ring-leaders, and those who had been guilty of committing murders, arson, and other heinous acts. The proclamation ran as follows: "In as much as it appears that amongst the Santals, who have risen in rebellion against the Government, plundering and devastating the country and opposing the troops, there are many who see the folly and iniquity of their proceedings, and are desirous of being pardoned and resuming their former life, notice is hereby given, that the Government, ever anxious for the welfare of its subjects though led away by counsels of bad men, will freely pardon all Santals who may within ten days appear before any constituted authority and tender their submission, always excepting those who shall be proved to have been principal

[223] *Ibid*

instigators and leaders of the insurrection, and those who shall be proved to have been principally concerned in the pepetration of any murder. As soon as complete submission is shown, all well-grounded complaints preferred by the Santals will be enquired into. But, on the other hand, all insurgents remaining in opposition will be visited with the promptest and severest punnishment." [224]

Apprehension of Fresh Outbreaks by the Lieutenant-Governor

The disturbances caused by the Santal insurgents in Birbhum seemed to have subsided in the month of August. The Magistrate of Birbhum reported on the 24th August, 1855: " All has been quiet for seven weeks past. The villagers have returned to their homes, and the husbandmen are engaged in the cultivation of their land as usual. The Santals are nowhere to be found......having retreated to a place some thirty miles off, in another district." [225] But Mr. Frederick James Halliday rightly apprehended that the Santals had retired " without any signs of General submission," and that on " three sides of the Hills " they were "likely to take advantage of the enforced and unavoidable inactivity of the troops to renew the attacks on the inhabitants of the open country." [226] He received a deputation from Messrs. Nelson & Co., the contractors for the Rajmahal line of the E. I. Ry., representing that great consternation prevailed in that neighbourhood among the Europeans as well as Indians, and that it would be difficult to recommence the construction of railways, which had been interrupted during the insurrection, " unless very active measures be taken to preserve the peace." [227]

[224] A Bengali version of it is preserved in the Record Office of the Deputy Commissioner of Santal Paraganas. *Vide* Appendix C.

[225] Letter to the Commissioner, dated the 24th August, 1855, para. 2, referred to by Hunter in *The Annals of Rural Bengal*, p. 249.

[226] The Lieutenant-Governor's Minute, dated the 12th September, 1855. *Vide* Appendix D.

[227] *Ibid.*

He granted Mr. Nelson permission to use 50 muskets and ammunition, and to "arm men whom he intended to entertain for the defence of his people and works and the neighbouring villages," [228] and undertook to provide him with arms.

As we find in the Lieutenant-Governor's Minute of the 12th September, 1855, he became rather anxious for the future safety and defence of the affected areas against renewed outbreaks. He considered it "impossible to make other than a partial and incomplete defence by means of the troops," [229] and suggested that a temporary force, "armed with matchlocks when such men are procurable or with muskets where men are to be had capable of using such arms," [230] be raised "to use it in guarding outlying villages distant from Military supports and also in patrolling between the several Military stations and especially along the line of Railroad under construction." [231] To facilitate communications between the military stations, especially along the line of railway works, he considered it necessary that the deep *nullahs* on the roads 'might be roughly bridged and the roads made fairly passable at a comparatively small expense," [232] and asked Messrs. Nelson & Co. to state the rate of cost per mile at which they were willing to undertake the work. He emphasised the need of extending the Electric Telegraph line, already established between Calcutta and Murshidabad, to Nalhati on the E. I. Ry. Loop line, and thence along that line to Rajmahal, Bhagalpur, Monghyr, and Patna. "It would be," he believed, "of the greatest advantage during the expected operations of the cold weather against the Santals and it would be withdrawn when the Railway was completed." [233] He asked the opinion of the Special Commissioner for the suppression of the

[228] *Ibid.*

[229] *Ibid.* Owing to the inclemency of the season, Major-General Lloyd had withdrawn the troops from the jungles, and had posted them " at such places as appeared best suited on the whole to protect the country round the Hills from the incursions of the Santals and at the same time to preserve the health of the Troops themselves."—*Ibid.*

[230] *Ibid.* [231] *Ibid.* [232] *Ibid.* [233] *Ibid.*

Santal insurrection, on the subject of disarming the Santals, by taking away from them their battle-axes, swords, bows, and arrows, before enacting a law to that effect, but ordered that "no time should be lost in bringing to trial the Santal prisoners who have been taken and the Special Commissioners should see to this. The Zila Magistrates will take up the cases on the prosecution of the Government represented by the Special Commissioners and their assistants." [234]

Reply of the Special Commissioner, Mr. A. C. Bidwell, to the Lieutenant-Governor

A copy of the Lieutenant-Governor's Minute, dated the 12th September, 1855, was sent to Mr. A. C. Bidwell, who expressed his opinions on different points contained in it, through his letter to the Bengal Government, dated the 22nd September, 1855.[235] He believed that there was "no fear of the upper part of the (Bhagalpur) District being disturbed by insurgent Santals," and that in course of two months more, the southern portion of the district, on the borders of Birbhum, where the Santal insurgents had assembled, would "be equally free from them." So, he did not think it necessary to maintain a temporary force, which, he remarked, could not be organised in that district in such a short time without considerable difficulty. He noted, however, that, in order to prevent "alarm of insurgents," he would consult General Lloyd "on the propriety of placing a military post somewhere about Sikree in addition to one at Pealapur (Pyalapore) as protection to the railway works in that neighbourhood......... and would also, as an additional encouragement, supply a limited number of muskets and ammunition to the contractors sufficient to defend, in case of necessity, each railway station on the line." He had "no objection whatever to the Government incurring a moderate expense in bridging the road...... along the projected

[234] *Ibid.*

[235] *Vide* Appendix E.

Railway." He believed that though there was no longer any need of such a road "as a means of communications between the military posts," it would "remain available to the public after the completion of the Railway, when it will continue to be a source of great convenience to the neighbouring villages." He was in favour of disarming the Santals, but intended to make further enquiries, and consider the matter more carefully, before recording fully his opinions on the matter. He promised to arrange for speedy trials of the Santal prisoners, but pointed out that the difficulty in the matter of "procuring the attendance of witnesses" might cause some delay.

Recrudescence of the Outbreak

The Lieutenant-Governor's apprehension was justified. The insurgents set at defiance the proclamation of pardon, and the insurrection broke out again in full fury within a month. The Magistrate of Birbhum wrote to the Commissioner of Burdwan on the 24th September, 1855: "During the past fortnight, upwards of thirty villages have been plundered and burned by the insurgents in Thannahs Operbundah (Operbandhah) and Nangoolea (Langulia). The whole of the country from Lorojore, four miles west of Nuggur (Nagore), to within a short distance of Deoghur, is in their hands. The Dawks (mails) are stopped; and the inhabitants deserted their villages and fled. They are divided into two large bodies; one encamped at Raksadangal, ten miles north of the Operbandah Thannah in Zillah Bhagalpore, and the other at Teelaboonie, six miles west of Soory, and also in Bhagalpore, but on the confines of Thannah Nangoolea (Langulia); and their numbers average, as nearly as we can ascertain, from 12,000 to 14,000, and are receiving augmentations from all quarters." A party of about 3,000 of the Raksadangal Santals, led by Mocheea Kosnjola, Rama, and Soondra Manjhis, encamped near Operbandhah in the evening of the 16th September, and on the next day plundered and burnt that village, and the local *thana*. A gang of 5,000 to 7,000 Santals under Seeroo Manjhi, who had taken Sooleah Thakur along with them, "strengthened their position by earthworks, and dug tanks there." To celebrate the Durga Puja festival there, they "carried off and detained two Brahmins from one of the villages plundered by them in Thannah Nangoolea." They waited for effecting a junction with the Raksadangal gang before attacking Suri. But, according to their usual practice, they had given intimation of their intended attack on Suri by sending there, through one of the Deoghur dak-runners, what was called in their language a '*ḍahra*' or missive, *viz.*, "a twig of the *Sāl* tree with three leaves on it, each leaf signifying a day that is to elapse before their arrival."[236] One Daroo Manjhi, son of Fagu Manjhi of Jagadispur under Thana Langulia in Birbhum, plundered the village of Banskuli in Birbhum, inflicting injuries on Petambar Mandal and some others, on the 5th of Sraban, 1262 B. S. at 1-30 P.M.[237] In the month of Kārtik, 1262 B. S. (October, 1855), Sidhu, Kanhu, Chand, and Bhairab, with about 200 Santals, plundered *mauja* Amba Harna in Tappa Belpatta (in the south of the Dumka sub-division) of the Bhagalpur District, and murdered three Bengalees there. Disturbances took place also at Jaypore, Kedra, Nonihat, and several other places in southern Bhagalpur.[238]

Additional Measures for the Supression of the Insurrection

Additional measures for the suppression of the insurrection were sanctioned by the Government from time to time. The

236 All these facts have been collected from the letter of the Magistrate of Birbhum to the Commissioner of the Burdwan Division, dated the 24th September, 1855.

237 A copy of the proceedings of the case of Daroo Manjhi, who was made over on the 14th December, 1855, to take his trial in the Sessions Court of Birbhum, is preserved in the Record Office of the Deputy Commissioner of Santal Paraganas. It may be noted here that Captain Halliday laid his camp near Banskuli.—Letter from Captain Halliday to Mr. A. R. Thompson, acting Magistrate of Birbhum, dated the 9th October, 1855.

238 Calcutta Review, 1856.

Government of India gave its consent to the plans of the temporary employment, with effect from the 14th July, 1855, of an extra police [239] force at a cost of Rs. 723 per mensem, and the establishment of temporary police *paharas* (watchmen)[240] at Nagore and Dubrajpur in Birbhum at a cost of Rs. 78 a month.[241] It also sanctioned the temporary engagement, with effect from the 24th September, 1855, of the *barkandaz* force formed by Mr. Ward when he was on special duty at Raniganj.[242] These extra police establishments were required " to afford assistance to the people in the disturbed state of the district of Beerbhum (Birbhum) by employing the force armed in guarding outlying villages distant from military support and in patrolling between the several military stations." [243]

Proclamation of Martial Law on the 10th November—its Effect

But even in the face of the renewed activities of the insurgents, the relations between the civil and military authorities continued to be rather strained, and misunderstandings frequently occurred between the two. This certainly affected the cause of the Government to a degree. A writer in the

[239]

No.	Post	Rs.
1	Sergeant in-Command	150
1	Jamadar	15
3	Daffadars at Rs. 10 each	30
66	Barkandazes at Rs. 8 each	528
		723

[240]

No.	Post	Rs.
2	Mohurers at Rs. 15 each	30
12	Barkandazes at Rs. 4 each	48
		78

[241] Letter from the Under-Secretary to the Government of Bengal to the officiating Commissioner of Burdwan, dated the 25th September, 1855. Proceedings No. 3541 of the Government of India's Financial Department, dated the 6th September, 1855.

[242] Letter from the Under-Secretary to the Government of Bengal to the officiating Magistrate of Birbhum, dated the 12th January, 1856.

[243] Proceedings of the Government of India in the Finance Department, dated the 22nd December, 1855.

Calcutta Review of 1855 expressed: "The confidence of our subjects in our rule is shaken, and in many parts they have undergone great suffering. A portion of the public is audibly grumbling at the apparent want of union and concert in the Government. Public money is melting away. Public works are at a standstill. Especially it is to be feared that the pet scheme of the day, the Railway, has received a serious check." In short, matters gradually took a serious turn, and the insurrection spread rapidly in different quarters. The Government, therefore, proclaimed Martial Law on the 10th November, 1855:—

"It is hereby proclaimed and notified, that the Lieutenant-Governor of Bengal, in the exercise of the authority given to him by Regulation X of 1804, and with the assent and concurrence of the President in Council, does hereby establish Martial Law in the following districts, that is to say: so much of the district of Bhagalpur as lies on the right bank of the river Ganges; so much of the district of Murshidabad as lies on the right bank of the river Bhagirathi; the district of Birbhum. And that the said Lieutenant-Governor does also suspend the functions of the ordinary criminal courts of judicature within the districts above described with respect to all persons, Santals and others, owing allegiance to the British Government in consequence of their either having been born or being residents within its territories and under its protection, who, after the date of this Proclamation and within the districts above described, shall be taken in arms in open hostility to the said Government or shall be taken in the act of opposing by force of arms the authority of the same, or shall be taken in the actual commission of any overt act of rebellion against the state;

"And that the same Lieutenant-Governor does also hereby direct that all persons, Santals and others, owing allegiance to the British Government who, after the date of his Proclamation, shall be taken as aforesaid, shall be tried by Court Martial; and it is hereby notified that any person convicted of any of the said crimes by the sentence of such court will be liable under Section 3, Regulation X of 1804, to the immediate punishment of death.''[244]

The proclamation of Martial Law encouraged the troops, stationed in different parts of the disturbed areas, to proceed vigorously with the work of chastising the Santal insurgents. They had no longer to suffer from the inclemency of the rainy season and the winter gave them a more suitable weather for active military operations. A number of outposts, sometimes consisting of twelve to fourteen thousand men, drove away the insurgents from the open country.[245] The Government then suspended the operation of Martial Law on the 3rd January, 1856.[246]

Disturbances After the Suspension of Martial Law

But after the suspension of Martial Law, certain parts of the country continued to remain disturbed for about three months more. Within a fortnight from the 3rd of January, 1856, fresh outrages were committed in the neighbourhood of Jaipur and on the Monghyr border by fugitive Santals from the south under the leadership of Saeb Shah. They abstained " from violence to human life and limb'' but plundered the European factory at Sangrampur (near Pakur) after sending manifestoes to the Government on the 12th and the 13th of January, 1856.[247] About the 14th of February, 1856, the *Daroga* of *thana* Dighee reported to Mr. W. C. Taylor, an Assistant Commissioner of Santal Paraganas stationed at Sreekoond (near Tinpahar), that about 6,000 or 7,000 ' armed Santals ' had gathered at Sorlah Pahar under Bijrit Parganait and Chortrea Nazir. The *Daroga*

244 Two contemporary Journals—the *Friend of India* of July-December, 1855, and the *Calcutta Review* of 1856—regretted " the delay in declaring Martial Law."

245 Letter from Brigadier L. S. Bird, Commanding the Birbhum and Bancorah (Bankura) frontier force, to the Collector of Birbhum, dated the 10th December, 1855.

246 Calcutta Review, 1856.

247 *Ibid.*

further reported that, on the 14th February, one of Mr. Pontet's *pyadas* (sepoys) went to a place called Baramasia (near about Barhait) to collect rents, when he was opposed by about 25 armed Santals, who had been "dressed in Red Saloo (a variety of cotton cloth), Pagrees (turbans) and had on white Lungies and long white Dhooties." These Santals declared before him: "The Ind (?) Sahib has excused the rents for this year, and if you say another word, we will kill you." They also discussed among themselves: "Let us go and seize the *Daroga* of Dighee and take him off to the Ind Sahib." On being informed of this, the *Daroga* of the said *thana* wrote to Mr. W. C. Taylor for urgent military aid, and the latter requested Major Gaussen, Commanding the 42nd Regiment N. I. at Barhait, to "send what he considered a sufficient force to the scene of disturbance with as little delay as possible." Mr. Pontet, who was then present near Major Gaussen, doubted the accuracy of the *Daroga*'s report, but, thinking it necessary to make proper enquiries, proceeded to Borio on the morning of the 16th February with one *Subahdar*, 2 *Havildars*, 2 *Naiks*, and 30 *sepoys*. On reaching Sorlith Pahar,[248] Mr. Pontet could "find no traces of the 6,000 or 7,000 insurgents which, he said, was all a myth of the Darogah's"[249] However, Mr. W. C. Taylor requested Major Gaussen "to station a detachment of his men" at Borio till the country was "in a more settled state,"[250] and Mr. Pontet's party remained at Borio for a few days before rejoining Major Gaussen's detachment at Barhait on the 24th February, 1856. Lieutenant Campbell, Commanding at Sreekoond, also sent 40 men to guard the railway officials at Seetapahar, lying about 8 miles north of Sreekoond.[251] Mr.

248 Letter from Major Gaussen to Captain B Parrot at Suri, dated the 13th February 1856 Letter from W. C. Taylor, Assistant Commissioner, Santal Parganas, dated the 16th February, 1856, to Mr A R. Thompson, Deputy Commissioner, Naya Dumka, paras. 6, 7, 8.

249 Letter from Major Gaussen to Captain B Parrot, dated the 13th February, 1856.

250 Letter from Mr. W. C Taylor to the Deputy Commissioner, Naya Dumka dated the 16th February, 1856.

251 *Ibid*, para 10

Taylor further suggested to the Deputy Commissioner at Dumka "the propriety of applying to Government for a detachment of at least 100 men to be established at Hiranpore," as there was no guard at Pakur, the Headquarters of that "division of the Railway and a place where there is always a large sum of money." Hiranpur, he believed, "would command Pakur and the whole of Umber (Ambar) which is entirely Santhalee (Santali) and the portions of Umber (Ambar) and Kankjole lying to the west of Haranpore in the Damin-i-koh and round about Mohul Bunnah (which) contain almost all the bad characters in this part of the country."[252] About the same time, the Deputy Commissioner of Santal Paraganas caused a number of proclamations to be distributed throughout his jurisdiction "prohibiting persons in the Damin-i-koh from having arms in their possession without a licence from the Deputy or Assistant Commissioner."[253]

Captain E. Sismore, officiating Principal Assistant to the Commissioner of Chotanagpur stationed at Hazaribagh, informed the Government of Bengal, on the 2nd March, 1856, that "in consequence of a large marauding party of Santals from the district of Birbhum having plundered several Mahajans near Serampore in Pergunnh Kurruckdeea" (*paragana* Khurruckdeah)[254] on the 21st and the 22nd February, he had detained a company of the 37th Regiment Native infantry for duty in that *paragana*, "the Police force having been inadequate to prevent a recurrence of similar outrages."[255] Captain E. Sismore was directed by the Lieutenant-Governor to "keep himself in communication"[256] with Brigadier L. S. Bird, who had been appointed to the special command of the troops engaged in the Bankura and Birbhum districts,* and with the Deputy Commissioner of the Santal Parganas. The 37th Regiment N. I. could not actually

[252] *Ibid*, para. 11.

[253] Letter from Mr. W. Grey, Secretary to the Government of Bengal, to Brigadier L. S. Bird, dated the 3rd March, 1856.

[254] *Ibid*. [255] *Ibid*. [256] *Ibid*.

send any detachment to Khurruckdeah,[257] and so Captain Sismore had to wait for the arrival of the 8th Regiment N. I., which having reached Burdwan on the 26th February had started for Dinapore on the 27th February and had come near Khurruckdeah by the beginning of March.[258] But in a day or two the Lieutenant-Governor found that it was no longer necessary to send any troops to Khurruckdeah.[259] All disturbances and panic soon subsided. Kanhu had been captured by the third week of February, 1856,[260] near Oparbandhab, north-east of Jamtara, by the Sardar *ghatwal* of Kunjra,[261] and was executed within a few days. A few other ring-leaders also met the same fate.

Trial and Punishment of the Santal Insurgents

The Editor of the *Friend of India* (July-December, 1855), and the *Calcutta Review* of (1856), advocated strong measures of punishment for the Santal insurgents. The former wrote: "It is only by striking terror into these blood-thirsty savages, who have respected neither age nor sex, that we can hope to quell this insurrection. It is necessary to avenge the outrages committed, and to protect the cultivators of the plains from a repetition of them. The Santals believe that they can enjoy the luxury of blood and plunder for a month without a certainty of retribution. It is absolutely necessary that this impression should be removed, or obliterated, if Government would not in these districts sit on bayonet points. To achieve this end, the retribution must be complete, leaving no calculation of chances for future rioters; so striking that none may fail to know and understand; and so tremendous that people may know their lives and happiness are not held of light account. It is to Pegu that we would convey the Santals, not one or two of the ring-leaders, but the entire

257 Letter from N W. Spottiswood, Commanding 37th Regiment N. I, to Captain E. Sismore, dated the 3rd March, 1856.

258 *Ibid*

259 Letter from the Under-Secretary to the Government of Bengal to Captain E. Sismore, dated the 5th March, 1856.

260 Letter from Mr. W. C. Taylor to Mr. A. R. Thompson, dated Sreekoond, the 20th February, 1856.

261 *Calcutta Review*, 1856.

population of the infected districts. India has not arrived at the point where armed rebellion can be treated with the contemptuous forbearance, with which an English Ministry can pardon a knot of Chartists or banish a gang of Irish patriots. Let the Santals' punishment be entrusted to a special commission as was done in Canada in 1838. Or even if this expedient be too arbitrary, let the villages be fined in an amount about equal to the plunder retained, and the sum distributed among the sufferers. To secure the punishment of the race, and restore the prestige of British authority, the mass of the Santals should not remain unpunished."

The Government, however, proceeded with cautious measures. A large number of Santal prisoners were regularly tried and convicted on charges of plunder, etc. There are two big files of cases of Santal prisoners in the Record Office of the Deputy Commissioner of Santal Paraganas. I find in one document that the Commisssioner of Santal Paraganas tried the cases of a large number of prisoners. These prisoners were originally 253 in number, but two of them were admitted as approvers during the trial. The remaining 251 (Santals 191, Nyas 34, Domes 5, Dhangers 6, Coles 7, Goala 1, Bhoeea 6, Rajwar 1) belonged to 52 different villages. Three among the 251 being released, the rest were found "guilty of the crime of plunder" by the Commissioner and his assessors, two of whom were Santals and "all of whom were men of intelligence." Among the 248 prisoners, there were 46 boys and youths of age ranging from 9 to 10 years, who "were given stripes of a rattan after the manner of school discipline" and were afterwards sent to their respective villages, four days' food being given to them. The rest of the prisoners were sentenced to long-term imprisonments, varying from seven to fourteen years. One Mirja Manjhi was tried and found guilty of "being an accomplice in plunder attended with murder of three persons at Koomrabad" (Kumrabad, now in the Dumka sub-division).[262]

[262] Letter from the Commissioner of Bhagalpur to Mr. A. R. Thompson, officiating Deputy Commissioner, Santal Paraganas, dated Camp Naya Dumka, the 14th February, 1856.

CHAPTER IV

SEQUEL TO THE INSURRECTION

This insurrection cannot be regarded as a mere local rising of no importance. For more than six months it remained a dreadful menace to the Government, the zamindars, and the people of the affected areas. Its suppression heavily taxed the energies of the troops as well as of the Government officers in several centres, such as Calcutta, Berhampore, Suri, Raniganj, Deoghur, Bhagalpur, Purneah, Monghyr, Barh, and Patna. The zamindars of different localities also co-operated in many ways with the Government. The insurrection further caused terrible losses both in men and money to, and seriously affected the revenues of, the Government.[263]

But good sometimes comes out of evil. This episode opened a new chapter in the history of Bengal and Bihar. It convinced the Government of the necessity of adopting prompt measures to bring the Santali areas under an effective administrative control. A ruler of Bengal cannot very well neglect the proper defence and administration of the areas covered by the Rajmahal Hills, because of their strategic and geographical importance. The Santal insurrection made the East India Company, then engaged in consolidating its hold on India, realise this fact fully. The Act 37 of 1855 formed the Santali areas into a separate non-regulation district, to be known by the general designation of the Santal Paraganas. This district, being placed under the control of the Commissioner of Bhagalpur, was divided into five jurisdictions.[264] These

263 Hunter, *Annals of Rural Bengal*, p. 253.

264 *Vide* Appendix G. Letter from Mr. Grey, Secretary to the Government of Bengal, to Mr. H. Steinforth, Commissioner of Bhagalpur, dated the 7th January, 1856. (The number and the area of the sub-divisions have been subsequently modified.)

were to be administered by the Deputy Commissioner (at Dumka) and four uncovenanted servants, to be called Assistant Commissioners ; and there was to be a Sub-Assistant Commissioner in each.[265] The Hon'ble Mr. (afterwards Sir) Ashley Eden, so long Assistant to the Special Commissioner for the suppression of the Santal insurrection, was appointed the first Deputy Commissioner on a monthly salary of Rs. 1,200. The salaries of the four Assistant Commissioners were settled as follows—of the first at the rate of Rs. 600, of the second at the rate of Rs. 500, and of the two others at the rate of Rs. 400 each per mensem. Of the Sub-Assistant Commissioners, one was to receive Rs. 200, two Rs. 150 each and two Rs. 100 each per mensem. There was to be a Sub-Assistant Surgeon at the Headquarters of the Deputy Commissioner and a native doctor at the Headquarters of each Assistant Commissioner.[266] Mr. W. C. Taylor was appointed an Assistant Commissioner for the Rajmahal area on a monthly salary of Rs. 600, with his Headquarters at Sreekoond (in Kankjole *paragana* under the Rajmahal sub-division)[267] ; Mr. J. M. G. Cheek of Bankura was made another Assistant Commissioner on a monthly salary of Rs. 100 ; and Mr. Browne Wood, Superintendent of salt *chowkies* (stations for collecting customs on all branches of trade), Jalasore Division, Contai, also became an Assistant Commissioner,[268] and Mr. R. E. Ronald of Tipperah was appointed the fourth Assistant Commissioner on a monthly salary of Rs. 400.[269] Mr. J. B. Shadwell of Cherapunji and Mr. R. G. Platts, Headmaster of Saran School, were appointed Sub-Assistant Commissioners on a monthly salary of Rs. 150 and 200 respectively[270] ; and Dr. Urquhart, F.R.C.S., was placed

[265] *Ibid.*

[266] *Ibid.*

[267] Letter from the Secretary to the Government of Bengal to Mr. W. C. Taylor, dated the 19th January, 1856.

[268] Letters from the Secretary to the Government of Bengal to Mr. J. M. G. Cheek and to Mr. Browne Wood, dated the 19th January. 1856.

[269] Letter from the Under-Secretary to the Government of Bengal to Mr. R. E. Ronald, Tipperah, dated the 25th February, 1856.

[270] Letter from the Under-Secretary to the Government of Bengal to Mr. J. B. Shadwell,

as the medical officer at the Headquarters of the district of Santal Paraganas on a monthly salary of Rs. 350. Mr. Eden soon resigned his post, and was succeeded (1856) by Mr. (afterwards Sir) Rivers Thompson.[271]

The Company's Government thus arranged for the efficient administration of the newly-formed district of Santal Paraganas. But the task before it was not a very easy one. The immediate effect of the movement on the economic condition of the Santals was terrible. Further, the Government had to think of the different classes of people, such as the Santals, the non-Santals, and the Pahariahs or hill-men. Mr. W. C. Taylor wrote from his Headquarters at Sreekoond to Mr. A R. Thompson, Deputy Commissioner of the Santal Paraganas, on the 4th April, 1856: "I think the great object at present is to prevent the Santals from starving; they have no seed for the season, nor is there any prospect of their getting any unless the Government comes forward with aid. Mahajans are not willing to trust the Santals with money to buy seed, and I would propose that a book should be opened in the office of each Assistant Commissioner, for registering all loans lent to Santals; and that Government should guarantee the repayment of the loans with interest at 24 per cent. as the Mahajans will not come forward if only allowed 12 per cent., and I think the Santals will be quite willing to pay the former amount of interest as they have hitherto been accustomed to pay 2 hundred or 300 per cent. . . . .

"The Pahariahs pay no revenue for their lands and the Sardars, Naibs and Manjhees (*Manjhis*) are bound to render every assistance to the police, and report at once the commission of crimes.

"The conduct of these men was anything but satisfactory during the insurrection and I would recommend that (they)......

dated the 25th February, 1856, and Letter from the same to Mr. R. G. Platts, dated the 29th March, 1856.

271 Letter from the Secretary to the Government of Bengal to Mr. A. R. Thompson, dated the 7th February, 1856.

should be forced to pay rent for their lands and put on the same footing as the Santals.

"There is no doubt that making the Pahariahs pay the rent would be beneficial to the country, as they would then be forced to pay more attention to the improvement and cultivation of their lands, than they do at present."

The officers placed in charge of the newly-created district, however, tried their best to settle the disturbed state of affairs. The Bengal Government sanctioned the establishment of grain-depots at Baunsi, Deoghur, and Naya Dumka, and passed orders against the practice of the sepoys "wandering over the country in search of Russud (provisions)."[272] Mr. W. C. Taylor tried, during the middle of February, 1856, to bring about uniformity in weights and measures by issuing *parwanahs* to the effect that, if, after the expiry of one month, the *baniahs* and others were "found selling or buying anything by any other weight than that of 80 tolas to the seer, they will be fined for the first offence Rs. 5, for the second offence Rs. 10 and for the third Rs. 25."[273] Improvements in general communications (roads, bridges, etc.), and in postal services, were also effected in different parts of the district.[274]

One of the important results of the Santal insurrection was the direction of missionary activities to the aboriginal races, in preference to the civilised people of the plains and towns of Bengal and Bihar. From this time, Chotanagpur, and the adjoining hill-districts of Bengal, became studded with missions. The political aspect of this work is that rude tribes have been taught the value of British contact and civilisation, and together with the policy of favourable and special treatment of aborigines and converted Christian aborigines, this

[272] Letter from Mr. W. Grey, Secretary to the Government of Bengal, to Brigadier L. S. Bird, Commanding Field Force, Soorie (Suri), dated the 15th February, 1856.

[273] Letter from Mr. W. C. Taylor to Mr. A. R. Thompson, dated Sreekoond, the 20th February, 1856.

[274] Letter from Brigadier L. S. Bird to the Secretary to the Government of Bengal, dated Camp Soorie (Suri), the 29th February, 1856.

made aboriginal discontent a very remote possibility. It is interesting to note that Indian reforming sects, as also orthodox Hindus and Muslims, have now applied the instrument of conversion to the aborigines, following the example of the Europeans, the result being a continuous absorption of the aborigines into Aryan-speaking Hindu or other communities.

Grant of Gratuities to the Relatives of the Murdered Darogas and Barkandazes

After the suppression of the insurrection, the relatives and heirs of those policemen who had been killed in course of it, applied to the Government for gratuities. Mahesh Datta, *daroga* of *thana* Dighee, who died after 20 years' service, left behind his widow named Seetalbati and two infant daughters[275]; Munno *barkandaz*, of the same *thana*, left behind a widow named Boodhoo and a son aged 5 years named Lutf Ali; Megboo *barkandaz*, also of the same *thana*, left behind his widow named Genda and two daughters; and Partabnarain, *daroga* of *thana* Kulhurrea, who died after 23 years' service, left behind his widow name Pearo, two daughters named Genda (12 years of age) and Sona (9 years of age), and a nephew named Hurruckchand.[276] Before granting any pecuniary support in the shape of gratuities to the petitioners, the Bengal Government asked the Commissioner of Bhagalpur and Santal Paraganas "to make particular enquiry as to the circumstances of their families"[277] and to inform the Lieutenant-Governor of the amount of gratuity he would recommend in each case.[278] We find that according to the orders of the Commissioner of Bhagalpur and

275 Petition of Seetalbati, *vide* Appendix H and Appendix I.

276 Letters from the Magistrate of Bhagalpur to the Commissioner of Bhagalpur, dated the 26th January, 1856 and the 12th December, 1857.

277 Letters from the Junior Secretary to the Government of Bengal to the Commissioner of the Bhagalpur Division and Santal Paraganas, dated the 11th March and the 20th August, 1857.

278 *Ibid.*

Santal Paraganas, dated the 1st September, 1857, the Magistrate of Bhagalpur submitted the following report regarding the petitioners, on the 12th October, 1857 : " Pertabnarain, Naib Suzawal, has left two daughters named Genda aged 12 years and Sona aged 9 and a nephew Hurruckchand, who has frequently held acting appointments in the Police but is at present out of employ. The two daughters are supported by him but as he is dependent on the chance of being nominated to temporary vacancies they cannot be considered as in easy circumstances. Muhesh Dutta is reported by the Deputy Magistrate of Barh to have left his family in easy circumstances. Meghoo Burkundaz's family appear to be proper objects for relief. The Magistrate of Bihar writes that from the reports of the Parganas of Thana Bihar it appears that since the death of Meghoo Burkundaz, resident of Mahallah Bhainsa Soor in the town of Bihar, his wife and two daughters (one still unmarried) are in great distress for want of necessary subsistence. They support themselves by begging. Sheik Munnoo Burkundaz has left a wife named Boodhoo and a son aged 5 years named Lootf Ali. She supports herself by spinning." [279] These facts were reported by the Commissioner of Bhagalpur and Santal Paraganas to the Bengal Government on the 20th February, 1858, and the latter solicited, on the 3rd of March, 1858, sanction of the Government of India " to the grant of gratuities to the surviving relatives " of one Naib Suzawal and two *barkandazes*. The Home Department of the Government of India referred the matter to the Council of India in the Financial Department, whereupon, according to number 6 of the gratuity rules, dated the 14th August, 1857, the Hon'ble the President in Council was " pleased to sanction the grant to the surviving relatives of a Naib Suzawal (Mahesh Dutta) and two Burkundazes (Munnoo and Meghoo), who were murdered at the

279 Thus it will be seen that the old practice of women supporting themselves by spinning did not disappear even then.

commencement of the Santal insurrection of 1855, of a gratuity equal to 6 months' pay of each of the deceased servants as shown below: 1st. To the 2 daughters of the Naib Suzawal whose salary in 1855 is understood to have been Rs. 12-8 per month—a gratuity of Rs. 75. 2nd. To the family of the 2 Burkundazes whose pay was Rs. 3 per month each—a gratuity of Rs. 18 each." [280]

280 Proceedings of the Honourable the President of the Council of India in the Financial Department, under date the 3rd April, 1858.

APPENDICES

APPENDIX A

The non-hilly tracts of the modern district of Santal Paraganas, included within *sarkar* Orambar or Tanda of the Bengal *subah* and comprising the *paraganas* of Sultanabad (now in the possession of the Maheshpur Raj), Ambar (now in the possession of the Pakur Raj), and Kankjole (in the south of the Rajmahal sub-division), and certain other portions of the Rajmahal, Jamtara and Deoghur sub-divisions, were brought under the effective control of the Mughals. The region up to Teliagarhi, which was regarded as 'the key of Bengal,' formed part of the Bengal *subah* and fell within the jurisdiction of *sarkars* Jennatabad or Lakhnauti and Orambar or Tandah. *Sarkar* Orambar stretched from the southern boundary of *sarkar* Purniah "southwards across the Ganges, all along the right bank of that river down to the city of Murshidabad on the one hand, through nearly the whole of the Birbhum district on the other. How far it may have penetrated into the hilly country on the west it is impossible to determine but probably some, at least, of the parganahs, now no longer traceable, represent territory claimed and assessed (on paper) in these hills though not actually conquered."[1] Large portions of the modern Pakur and Rajmahal sub-divisions were included within the *mahals* or *paraganas* of Ambar, Kankjole, and Sultanabad of this *sarkar*. Hamilton Buchanan, who surveyed the Bhagalpur district in 1809-11 A.D., has left detailed accounts of these *paraganas*. *Sarkar Purniah* "comprised only the central portion of the present district of the same name.

[1] "Notes on Akbar's Subahs, with reference to the Ain-i-Akbari," by John Beames, B.C.S., in the *Journal of the Royal Asiatic Society*, 1896.

Parganah Dharampur—a long strip on the west and south—belonged to *subah* Bihar ; another long strip on the south was divided between *sarkars* Audambar (Orambar), Lakhnauti, and Tajpur ; all the lands east of the Mahananda river were in Tajpur ; and the northern part of the district was yet unconquered." [2] But, at the same time, a study of the boundary of *sarkar* Mungher (modern Monghyr), as given in the *Ain-i-Akbari,* would show that this *sarkar* ran far down southwards into the jungle tracts, now in the Santal Paraganas,[3] but it is not possible " to fix any definite boundaries in that direction. Probably the Muhammadans did no more than make occasional raids into this wild and difficult country............" [4] While mentioning the *faujdari* divisions of Bengal and Bihar, Ghulam Husain, the author of *Siyar-ul-mutakherin,* includes Rajmahal and Purniah within the jurisdiction of the Bengal *subah.*[5] " In the year 1728 the zamindari of Rajshahi extended from Bhagalpur on the west to Dacca on the east, and included a large sub-division called Nil Chakla Raj Shahi, which stretched across Murshidabad and Nadia as far as the frontiers of Birbhum and Burdwan." [6] The extent of this zamindari was gradually reduced since the last quarter of the 18th century.

Major James Rennell, who conducted surveys of Bengal and Bihar between 1763-70 A.D., includes certain parts of modern Santal Paraganas (now in the Deoghur, Jamtara and Dumka sub-divisions of this district) in Birbhum.[7] These were (*i*) Belpatta, originally forming a part of *sarkar* Orambar of Bengal ; (*ii*) the large *paragana* of Sarath-Deoghur, now forming the Deoghur sub-division ; (*iii*) the *paraganas* of Kundahit,

[2] Journal of the Royal Asiatic Society, 1896, p. 90.

[3] This is corroborated by the authors of *Haft-i-Aqalım* (an 18th century work) and *Haq-i-Qatha-i-Hindustan* (also an 18th century work). The former also refers to the presence of mica mines towards the south in the hilly regions of this *sarkar,*

[4] Journal of the Asiatic Society of Bengal, 1885, Part I, p. 172.

[5] *Siyar-ul-mutakherin* (English translation), Vol. III, p. 179.

[6] Imperial Gazetteer, Vol. XXI, p. 162.

[7] Journals of Major James Rennell.

Karaya and Pabbia, now comprising the Jamtara sub-division, (*iv*) Kumrabad (25 miles N.W. of Suri, the Headquarters of the Birbhum district), now in the south of the Dumka sub-division ; (*v*) Muhammadabad, now in the Dumka sub-division and belongs to the Hetampur Raj. Belpatta was transferred to the Bhagalpur district in 1781 on the recommendation of Mr. Cleveland. When Hamilton Buchanan made a survey of the Bhagalpur district, during 1809-11 A.D., he saw Belpatta included in it. The Bhagalpur district, as Buchanan saw it, also extended over *paraganas* Ambar, Sultanâbad, a part of Kankjole and certain other *paraganas*, originally belonging to *sarkars* Orambar and Jennatabad. Of these, certain places like Pratapganj, Aurangabad, and Farrukhabad (all situated near Dhulian), then included in the Bhagalpur district, now lie in the Murshidabad district of Bengal.

APPENDIX A 1

From Mr. J. Allen, Commissioner of Chotanagpur, to William Grey, Esquire, Secretary to the Government of Bengal, Fort William, dated Hazaribagh, the 17th December, 1855 :—

I do myself the honour to report that I have made very careful enquiries, both public and private, at Hazaribagh regarding the statement made by the Santal prisoner Runjeet Manjee (Ranjit Manjhi), charging the Ex-Amir, Meer Abbas Ali Khan, with being concerned in the Santhál rebellion.

2. I have not been able to obtain evidence or information which leads me to believe or suspect that Meer Abbas Ali Khan has been guilty of any direct or indirect participation in the Santhal insurrection.

3. The Ameer like others of his race is passionately fond of the pleasures of the chase, and maintained while he resided at Hazareebagh (Hazaribagh) a large hunting Establishment. He had in his service many professional hunters of all castes, among whom was the Santhal Manjhee Urjoon who is mentioned

in the statement of the Prisoner Runjeet Manjee as one of the originators of the Santhal Disturbances.

4. This Urjoon has been apprehended by my orders but unfortunately he effected his escape close to the station of Hazaribagh from the persons sent by the Principal Assistant Commissioner to bring him in. I have offered a reward of 5 rs. for him, and if the police exert themselves he ought to be re-apprehended in a few days.

5. The hunting parties of the Ameer were conducted on a large scale according to the custom of his country. A thousand or sometimes as many as 2,000 Jungle beaters were collected together on those occasions, a very large portion of these were Santhals from the Ramgurh and Khurruckdeah hills who are almost all skilful hunters.

6. Urjoon Manjhee, as a servant of the Ameer, was a person of some consequence among the Ramgurh Santhals, his family reside in the Pulgunge Division Pergunnah Khurruckdeah, and through them he had some influence also with the Khurruckdeah Santhals, for this reason he was employed by the Ameer to assemble the Santhal beaters for his hunting expeditions. These Santhals came not only from Ramgurh and Khurruckdeah Pergunnahs, but sometimes on grand occasions from the neighbourhood of Deogarh and from the villages of the Bhagalpur and Beerbhum Districts which are contiguous to the boundaries of the South-West Frontier Jurisdiction.

7. About the middle of April last (the 11th and 12th I think are the dates) the Ameer had a grand hunting party at Nurkundie (not Burokondie as stated by Ranjit Manjee). There were I understand about 1,500 beaters engaged on this occasion, about two-thirds of whom were probably Santhals. This evidently is the Shikar party referred to by the Prisoner Runjeet Munjee, for I find that the Ameer had no other large shooting party in the month of April or about that time. The Hazareebagh Cutchery being closed for the Churruck Poojah holidays the Ameer invited Mr. W. C. Spencer the officiating Principal

Assistant and Dr. Kelley the Civil Assistant Surgeon to join his party and both these gentlemen were with the Ameer from the beginning to the end of the shooting excursion.

8. If the Ameer had any treasonable intentions, had he assembled those Santhals with the view of instigating them to rebellion, it is not probable that these two gentlemen would have been invited to his Camp, and had any communication of this kind been made to these Santhals, it is likely that either Mr. Spencer or Dr. Kelley or some of their servants would have heard something about the matter.

9. Urjoon Manjee does not bear a good character; he is a violent man and addicted to drink. In February last the Ameer discovered that this Santhal and one of his Scindian servants had been oppressing the Ryots of some of the villages which he used to frequent for shooting purposes and he sent them both to the Principal Assistant Commissioner at Hazareebagh requesting that they might be punished; on the 24th of March last Urjoon Manjee and Metho were sentenced by the Principal Assistant Commissioner to 15 days' imprisonment, and to a fine of 25 rs. each or a further imprisonment of 15 days with labour which was commutable to a fine of 10 Rupees. Against this order the Defendants appealed to the Deputy Commissioner but their appeal was rejected, and they were released from jail at the expiration of their sentence on the 24th of April, 1855.

10. At the time therefore of the Nurkundee shooting party Urjoon Manjee was a Prisoner in the Hazaribagh jail. Under these circumstances it is in my opinion highly improbable that the Ameer should have taken these proceedings against his Santhal servant and thus excited his animosity, had he made or intended to make use of him as an instrument in any insurrectionary movement.

11. I ought not to omit to mention that at these hunting parties the Dependants and servants of the Maharajah of Ramgurh were always present, and generally the Ameer entrusted the payment of the Santhal beaters to them. If a conspiracy on a large scale

was being hatched at any of these shooting parties the Ramgurh Rajah's people must have been cognisant of it and they are not likely to have concealed it from their Master. The Ramgurh Rajah has always shown himself to be a loyal and well-conducted chief and I am satisfied that he would not in any way have connived at a plot of this kind.

12. Amongst the witnesses that I have examined at Hazareebagh, was a Santhal named Purthee, a nephew of Urjoon Manjee; he was brought to me and I took his evidence before he had time to communicate with any one; he is a simple country lad of about 19 or 20 years of age, and spoke out frankly as the Santhals generally do when kindly spoken to and when they have nothing to fear or to conceal. He stated that in August and September, 1854, about 10 Santhals from a distant part of the country came to Urjoon's house in Mouza Durmiah Pergunnuh Jugasee, the names of five of them were Sedhoo Manjee, Kanhoo Manjee, Sonah Manjee, Sormah Manjee, and Urjoon Manjee; the names of the five others he did not know. The strangers complained, that they had been obliged to abscond from their homes on account of the tyranny and oppression of the Mahajans, who under the pretence of having lent them money had plundered all their property. Urjoon Manjee offered to get his Master, Meer Abbas Ali Khan, to interest himself in their favour, and he went or pretended to go to Hazareebagh to see the Ameer on the subject, leaving the Santhals at his house. He remained absent for 3 days, and on his return home told the strangers that he had brought a letter from the Ameer ordering their property to be given up to them.

* * * *

14. This is the only fact I have been able to elicit which tends in any way to connect the Ameer with those who have been in rebellion, but I am bound to observe that I have very little dependence upon anything that Urjoon Manjee may have told these stranger Santhals, for it is much more likely that

he falsely stated that he brought an order from the Ameer than that the Ameer should have given an order to persons whom he had never seen and over whom he had no influence or control.

15. Urjoon Manjee formerly resided at Chummerkoh (or Churneer Koh) in Pergunnuh Khurruckdeah, his two brothers (Kieroo Manjee and Intee Manjee) and other members of his family are the inhabitants of that village, he is said to be distantly connected with Kanoo, Seedhoo, and Bhyrow, the leaders of the Santhal insurrection ; he is just the sort of man with whom evil-disposed persons would be likely to communicate if they wished to excite the Insurrection he is a determined and reckless man, he is not wanting in intelligence, and has some influence with the Hazareebagh Santhals.

16. After a careful enquiry I have arrived at the conclusion, that Meer Abbas Ali Khan has not had anything to do with this insurrection. . . .

17. I think it not improbable that Urjoon Manjee may have listened to the overtures of the Bhagalpur and Beerbhum rebels and that he may have made use of the Ameer's name to encourage them but it does not appear that he has been absent from his house and the neighbourhood since the insurrection commenced or has taken any active part in the Bhagalpur and Beerbhum disturbances.

APPENDIX B

ধর্ম্মাবতার জয়তি।

পাহাড়ীয়া সাঁওতালগণ জমা হওয়া বিষয় বিস্তারিত গতকল্য হুজুরে নিবেদন করিয়াছি—অন্ত থানা সুরাইর গণেস সিংহ বরকন্দাজ পাকর মোকাম হইতে অত্র থানায় পঙঁছিয়া বরাবর কাচারির মধ্যে অধিন নিকট বাচনিক অন্ত দিবা একপ্রহর সময় আন্দাজ ৫০০০ হাজার সাঁওতাল তির খামচা টেঙ্গা তলওয়ার ডঙ্কা দিয়া চারিখানা পাল্কী সঙ্গে পাকোরী রাজধানীতে পহুঁছিয়া রাজধানী ও পাকুরী গ্রাম লুট করা সচক্ষে দেখাদী প্রকাশ করিল—কিন্তু পাকোরী মোকাম

অত্র থানা হইতে ৫ ক্রোশ ব্যবধান—এদেশে আই যাই অধিক নাই এবং রেলওয়ে সাহেব লোক যে প্রকার ব্যস্ত হইয়া জিনিষপত্র লইয়া পলাইতেছে তাহা দেখিয়া এদেহাতের প্রজালোক অনেক পলাইতেছে এমত অবস্থায় উক্ত কাকেলা সাঁওতাল এদেশে পহুঁছিলে লুট হওয়া সম্ভব—অধিন শকল শহীত শতক্য থাকায় হুজুরের গোচরার্থে নিবেদন করিল ধর্ম্মাবতার কর্ত্তা নিবেদনমিতি

১৮৫৫।১২ জুলাই।

[Copy preserved in the office of the Deputy Commissioner of Santal Paraganas, Dumka.]

APPENDIX C

Proclamation, dated the 17 August, 1855 (in Bengali) :—

………রাজবিদ্রোহ কর্ম্ম করিয়া অত্র দেশ লুট ও উজার করিতেছে—আর সৈন্যের সহিত আপত্য করিতেছে—উহারদিগের মধ্যে এমত অনেক ব্যক্তী আছে জে আপনাদিগের নির্ব্বুদ্ধি ও দুষ্কর্ম জ্ঞান করিয়া মার্জ্জনা ও পূর্ব্ব-কারাবস্থা পুনরায় পাইবার প্রার্থী আছে—এ বিষয় ইস্তাহার দেওয়া যাইতেছে যে গভর্ণমেণ্ট সর্ব্বদা আপনার প্রজার সুখ…………তাহারা মন্দলোকের পরামর্শে কুপথগামী হয় ইচ্ছুক নয় এ নিমিত্ত কেবল এই সকল ব্যক্তী জাহারা প্রধান মন্ত্রী ও সরদার কিম্বা কোন খুন করিতে প্রাধান্যরূপে অধিক থাকা প্রকার হইবেক তদ্ব্যতিরিক্ত সকল সাঁওতালগণ জাহারা ১০ দশ দিবসের মধ্যে কোন হাকিমের সম্মুখে হাজীর হইয়া আজ্ঞাবাহী হইবেক তাহাদিগের দোশ মার্জ্জনা করা জাইবেক—জখন তাহাদের আজ্ঞাবাহী যুক্ত প্রকাশ হইবে তখন তাবত নালিশ সাঁওতালদিগের যাহা প্রমাণযোগ্য হইবেক তাহা সুন্দররূপে তদারক করা যাইবেক কিন্তু যত্তপি সকল রাজদ্রোহি এই ইস্তাহার জারির পর বিপরিত আচরণ করে তাহার সক্ত ও নিদারুণ সাজা পাইবেক। ইতি সন ১৮৫৫ সাল—তাঃ ১৭ই আগষ্ট—মোতাক সন ১২৬২ সাল—২ ভাদ্র।

[Copy preserved in the office of the Deputy Commissioner of Santal Paraganas, Dumka.]

APPENDIX D

The Lieutenant-Governor's Minute, dated the 12th September, 1855 :—

Since that time there have been appearances of renewed outbreak, and I append to this Minute extracts of letters just received from Messrs. Bidwell and Ward and a copy of a letter written to Mr. Nelson the contractor by one of his agents near Rajmahal which seem to show that on three sides of the Hills the Santhals are likely to take advantage of the enforced and unavoidable inactivity of the troops to renew the attacks on the inhabitants of the open country.

Against this it is I fear impossible to make other than a partial and incomplete defence by means of the troops. But assistance may be given to the people by means of temporary Police armed with matchlocks when such men are procurable or with muskets where men are to be had capable of using such arms. The attention of Messrs. Bidwell and Ward should be directed to this and they should be requested to make exertions to raise a temporary force such as above described and to use it in guarding outlying villages distant from Military supports and also in patrolling between the several Military stations and specially along the line of Railroad under construction.

From Pealapur (Pyalapore) to Rajmahal the line is necessarily left bare of troops because of the jungly nature of the road and country, and Mr. Bidwell should supply the gap, which is an important one, on account of the Railway works within it, by Police posts and Patrols of the nature above referred to.

The Commissioners will be careful to report without delay all expenses they may incur on this account in order that it may be submitted for sanction in proper form to the supreme Government.

I have received a deputation to represent on the part of Messrs. Nelson and Co., the contractors for the Rajmahal line, the great consternation which reigns in that neighbourhood among Europeans as well as Natives and the difficulty which will be experienced in recommencing the Railway works which have been interrupted during the insurrection unless very active measures be taken to preserve the peace. The deputation were well satisfied when made acquainted with the manner in which the troops are to be stationed and with the other proposed measures and they appeared to think then the present panic would soon subside when the purposes of Government are known.

Mr. Nelson was asked to be allowed to keep up the communications between the several Military posts, especially along the line of Railway works. This is at present interrupted by deep and difficult Nullahs and by the absence of almost all that can be called road.

With the aid of the contractors on the line who are very willing to assist in the business, the Nullahs might be roughly bridged and the roads made fairly passable at a comparatively small expense and I would call on Messrs. Nelson and Co., to state at what expense per mile they are willing to undertake the work.

Great inconvenience would result to the present operations and more especially to those which it appears too probable that we shall have to carry on with renewed vigour next cold season against the Santhals, if the Electric Telegraph now established between Calcutta and Murshidabad were not prolonged to Bhagalpur, General Lloyd's Headquarters. On the 24th ultimo I strongly recommended to the Government of India that there should be established a line of Electric Telegraph communication between Calcutta and Patna *via* Sherghatty. In reply on the 7th instant the Government of India has expressed doubts as to the necessity of incurring the expense of such a line seeing that the Railway Telegraph will ultimately (*i e.*, four or five years hence) pass through Patna and will be passed by an Electric Telegraph.

I have had to make several very important communications to Patna and Dinapore during the present insurrection and even before it, and I have been quite satisfied that the benefit to Government of an immediate communication with such important civil and military centres as Patna and Dinapore is likely to be of great and continual importance. At present when I have a communication to make to those places I am obliged to do it by Electric Telegraph to Sherghatty and thence by Express.

But if the line were now continued from Murshidabad to Nalhati (on the line of Rail-road now in construction) and thence along that line to Rajmahal, Bhagalpur, Monghyr and Patna, the communication between Calcutta and Patna would be established on the most comprehensive and beneficial footing. It would be of the greatest advantage during the expected operations of the cold weather against the Santhals and it could be withdrawn when the Railway was completed. To me indeed the need of such a communication seems so clear and pressing that I trust it will not be determined to postpone it until the somewhat indefinite period of the completion of the Railway to Patna.

From the contractors and Engineers employed on the Railway line and near the disturbed districts I have heard much of the importance of having a Deputy Magistrate stationed at Rajmahal and similar officers elsewhere within available distances along the Railway works, and some of the gentlemen employed on the line have expressed their willingness to be employed in the emergency as Magistrates.

I cannot but think it would be wise for the Government to avail itself of the assistance of the very respectable and energetic English gentlemen who are now employed in those parts of the country and who have in various instances during the late insurrection and consequent operations evinced great zeal, determination, judgment, disinterestedness and public spirit. On this subject I would desire to consult the Special Commissioner and the local authorities who should name such of the gentlemen alluded to as in their judgment may fitly be entrusted with the duties of Honorary Magistrates.

Great stress is laid on the necessity for disarming the Santhals by many persons who have been concerned in or interested in the operations for the suppression of the insurrection and I consider it a matter deserving of early and careful consideration. It is especially insisted on that the battle-axes, swords and bows and steel-tipped arrows of the Santhals should be taken from them and that as there are no Santhals in the Hills it will not be difficult to prevent their rearming themselves in future.

If done, this will require a law and I would ask the opinions of the Special Commissioners on the subject.

No time should be lost in bringing to trial the Santhal prisoners who have been taken and the Special Commissioners should see to this. The Zilla Magistrates will take up the cases on the prosecution of the Government represented by the Special Commissioners and their assistants.

APPENDIX E

Letter from Mr. A. C. Bidwell to the Bengal Government, dated the 22nd September, 1855 :—

My particular attention is first called to paras 5, 6 and 7 of the minute on which reference is made to the necessarily incomplete protection afforded to the country by the troops and the expediency impressed upon me of providing the people with assistance by means of temporary police armed with matchlocks or muskets to be used in guarding outlying villages and in patrolling between the several military stations, especially along the line of Railway Road under construction. The importance of supplying protection to the tract of country from Pealapoor (Pyalapore) to Rajmahal now left bare of troops is more particularly dwelt upon.

There would I fear be extreme difficulty in organising in this district and in a short space of time any police of the character described, who would at all enjoy the confidence of the community or repay the cost of their entertainment. I am happy to add however that as at present informed I can advise the Government that there is no necessity for their entertainment. The consternation described by the Railway contractors as reigning on the Rajmahal line amongst Europeans as well as natives to the best of my information no longer exists among the natives at any rate and the Police reports from all quarters comprised in a line drawn from Baousee (Baunsi) to Godda, from Godda to Rajmahal and from Rajmahal to Nulhati (Nalhati) agree in describing the country as entirely free from alarms on account of Santals.

The Dawk runners who are as timid as the workmen on the Railroad can possibly daily traverse the Damin from Mahgaon (Mahagama) through Borio to Rajmahal without alarm, and there had not once been an instance known of a body of Santals passing out between two military posts with a view of plundering the country outside.

I trust that the later accounts received from their Agents will have removed the alarm entertained by the Railway contractors. I am however fully alive to the necessity of preventing not only danger from but alarm of Insurgents and will consult General Lloyd on the propriety of placing a military post somewhere about Sikree in addition to one at Pealapur (Pealapore) as protection to the Railway works in that neighbourhood. I would also as an additional encouragement supply a limited number of muskets and ammunition to the contractors sufficient to defend in case of necessity each Railway station on the line.

But as I said before I consider them to be means of importing confidence rather than protection to the Railway operations for there is I think no fear of the upper part of this District being again disturbed by insurgent Santals and trust that in the course of two months more the southern portion where they are now located on the borders of Birbhum will be equally free from them.

As regards the measure referred to in paras 10 and 11 of His Honour's minute I see no objection whatever to the Government incurring a moderate expense in bridging the road which has been made by the contractors alongside the projected Railway. This road I conclude will remain available to the pubiic after the completion of the Railway, when it will continue to be a source of great convenience to the neighbouring villages, for its service as a means of communication between the military posts along the line has I trust gone by.

I entirely concur in the importance which is attached both by the Government and the contractors to the presence of a Deputy or Assistant Magistrate at Rajmahal and I think that no time should be lost in nominating one. He should be a European and thoroughly efficient officer and if no Deputy Magistrate of this description is available I would suggest the propriety of placing there a covenanted assistant with special powers.

As regards the advisability of vesting some of the gentlemen connected with the Railway with powers as Honorary Magistrates, I will as desired ascertain the views of the local authorities and report the result. I confess however that I see considerable difficulties in the matter and should be glad to hear something of the view of the Railway gentlemen themselves as to the mode in which their services as Honorary Magistrates can be brought into play and in what description of cases they propose to exercise these powers.

As at present informed I entirely concur in the necessity of disarming the Santals. I will however make further enquiries and consider the matter more carefully before recording fully my sentiments upon this subject. I am led to believe however that it is a mistake to suppose that there are no smiths in the Hills, but there ought nevertheless to be no difficulty in keeping this race unarmed if a law be passed on the subject.

The instructions regarding the speedy trial of the Santal prisoners shall be attended to but the difficulty which exists in procuring the attendance of witnesses will I fear prevent the early disposal of the cases.

APPENDIX F

List of Police Establishments in Zillah Bhagalpur Transferred to the Commissioner of the Santal Pergunnahs (*paraganas*) [1]

Thannah Lukerdewanee or Noni—							
Daroga	...	75	0	0			
Muhurrir	...	8	0	0			
Jamadar	...	8	0	0			
14 Barkandazes	...	56	0	0			
Paper, etc.	..	3	0	0			
					150	0	0
Thannah Colgong—							
Daroga	...	50	0	0			
Muhurrir	...	8	0	0			
Jamadar	...	8	0	0			
10 Barkandazes	...	40	0	0			
Paper, etc.	...	3	0	0			
					109	0	0
Chookee Pealapore—							
Jamadar	...	8	0	0			
					8	0	0
Thannah Pointee removed to Pursa—							
Daroga	...	50	0	0			
Muhurrir	...	8	0	0			
Jamadar	...	8	0	0			
10 Barkandazes	...	40	0	0			
Paper, etc.	...	3	0	0			
					109	0	0

[1] Letter from Mr. H. Richardson, Magistrate of Bhagalpur, dated the 4th March, 1856, to the Commissioner of Santal Parganas.

Gungapersad—

Jamadar	... 8	0	0			
6 Barkandazes	... 24	0	0			
Paper, etc.	... 1	0	0			
				33	0	0

Additional Thannah Sackrigully—

Jamadar	... 8	0	0			
6 Barkandazes	... 24	0	0			
Paper, etc.	... 1	0	0			
				33	0	0

Thannah Rajmahal—

Daroga	... 50	0	0			
Muhurrir	... 8	0	0			
Jamadar	... 8	0	0			
14 Barkandazes	... 56	0	0			
Paper, etc.	... 3	0	0			
				125	0	0

Thannah Fudkeepoor (Phudkipur)—

Daroga	... 50	0	0			
Muhurrir	... 8	0	0			
Jamadar	... 8	0	0			
14 Barkandazes	... 56	0	0			
Paper, etc.	... 3	0	0			
				125	0	0

Hill Thannah Digbee—

Naib Suzawal	... 12	8	0			
Muhurrir	... 7	0	0			
7 Barkandazes	... 21	0	0			
				40	8	0

Hill-Thannah Dumka—						
Naib Suzawal ...	12	8	0			
Muhurrir ...	7	0	0			
6 Barkandazes ...	18	0	0			
				37	8	0
Hill Thannah Kurhurrea—						
Naib Suzawal ...	12	8	0			
Muhurrir ...	7	0	0			
7 Barkandazes ...	21	0	0			
				40	8	0
Hill Thannah Rajmahal—						
Naib Suzawal ...	12	8	0			
Muhurrir ...	10	0	0			
Jamadar ...	8	0	0			
6 Barkandazes ...	18	0	0			
Umber—						
Jamadar ...	8	0	0			
5 Barkandazes ...	15	0	0			
				71	8	0
	Total ...			882	0	0

APPENDIX G[1]

Divisions of the Santal Paraganas

I have the honour to request that until experience shows the expediency of alteration the five Divisions of the Santal Pergunnahs (*paraganas*) may be as follows :—

Central Division

1. Pergunnah Hendwa } Bhagalpur.
2. Tuppeh Belputta }
3. ,, Mohomadabad } Birbhum.
4. Pergunnah Hareepur }
5. Tuppeh Inarpul of the Damin-i-koh.

[1] Letter from the Commissioner of Santal Paraganas, dated Camp Deoghur, the 11th March, 1856, to Mr. A. R. Thompson, officiating Deputy Commissioner, Santal Parganas.

North-Eastern Division (under Mr. Taylor).

1.	Pergunnah	Teleagurhee	Bhagalpur.
2.	,,	Jummonee	
3.	,,	Kankjole	
4.	,,	Bahadurpoor	
5.	,,	Chetowleah	
6.	,,	Akburnugger	
7.	,,	Sooltangunge	
8	,,	Huzzar Tukkee	
9.	,,	Inayat Nugger	
10.	,,	Muksaceu	
11.	,,	Mouzas of Thannah Rajmahal in the Damin-i-koh.	

South-Eastern Division

1.	Pergunnah	Umber	Bhagalpur.
2.	,,	Sooltanabad	
3.	,,	Durren Molissre	Birbhum.
4.	,,	Mallarpur	
5.	,,	Hooknapoor (N. of R. More)	
6.	,,	Nonee	
7.	Tuppeh Darpul in the Damin-i-koh.		

North-Western Division

1.	Pergunnah	Bhagalpur (See Act 37 of 1855)	Bhagalpur.
2.	,,	Colgong (See do)	
3.	,,	Godda	
4.	,,	Pussye	
5.	,,	Umlomotea	
6.	,,	Muneeares	
7.	The Mouzas of Thannahs Dighee and Kurhurrea in the Damin-i-koh.		

South-Western Division

1. Pergunnah Pubbea.
2. Tuppeh Kundit Kurayeh.
3. Sarath Deoghur ,,

APPENDIX H

FROM

The Junior Secretary to the Govt. of Bengal,

To

The Commissioner of the Bhagalpur Division.

Dated Darjeeling, the 11th March, 1857.

SIR,

I am directed by the Lieutenant-Governor to forward to you a copy of a petition professing to be from one Seetal Daye alias Rajcoomari, widow of Mohesh Dutt, Late Naib Suzawal of Thana Dighee, praying for support from Government for the family of her late husband in consideration of his having been killed in endeavouring to quell the disturbances among the insurgent Santhals and to request that you will submit a full report on the prayer of the petitioner stating especially whether the oppressive conduct of the deceased Naib Suzawal was not supposed to be in a great measure the cause of the late insurrection as well as of his murder.

Sd. Illegible,

Junior Secretary to the Govt. of Bengal.

APPENDIX I

To

The Secretary to the Government of Bengal with the
Lieutenant-Governor.

The humble petition of Mossammat Seetal Daye alias Rajcoomari widow of Mohesh Dutt, late Naib Suzawal of Thana Dighee, Zilla Bhagalpur, humbly sheweth :—

That your petitioner most respectfully begs the favour of your laying the following circumstances before his Honour the Lieutenant-Governor and of advocating on behalf of a poor widow now destitute of all means of support.

That her late husband Mohesh Dutt held the office of the Naib Suzawal of Thana Dighee in the Damin-i-koh from the year 1835 to 7th July 1855 a period of about 21 years, that sometime before the above date when he was on leave at home the Santhal insurrection broke out and he received a perwanah from Mr. Pontet then Superintendent of the Damin-i-koh to go and join his Thana and take steps for the suppression of the insurrection, that in obedience to Mr. Pontet's order he immediately proceeded to his Thana and learning that a great number of Santhals had assembled at a place near Putchkoteah (Panchkethia) he went to that village. In the next morning three of the Santhals came to him from an adjoining neighbourhood where the Santhals had assembled and desired him to go and visit their Thakur there. He lost no time to repair to the spot accompanied by a few Burkundazes but to his surprise found that the Santhals had bound down some of the Bengalee Mahajans and had already commenced practising great violence over them. That her husband the Suzawal tried his utmost to dissuade the insurgents from their oppressive conduct but in vain ; they declared that the British Government is no more, their (the Santhal) reign having already commenced. Subsequently they ordered him to collect 5 rupees from each of the

Mahajans to be given to them. On this the Suzawal told them he will be prepared to send from his Thana whatever sums they required but the Santhals declined and told him that they have understood that he would under this pretence quit the spot and report the matter to the Magistrate, and so Sidhu their chief killed the Suzawal and two other Burkundazes on the spot.

That her late husband has left his two infant daughters and family consisting of 4 other women quite unprotected and who have been now reduced to the utmost stage of poverty. Under these circumstances she has no other course open to her than to present this her humble petition earnestly expecting that a perusal of which will induce His Honour to grant a pension for the maintenance of the family of one who was killed while endeavouring to quell the insurrection and thereby save the lives of thousands.

That she has further been emboldened to present this petition on the ground that she in her present condition considers herself the fit object of pity and deserving of such indulgence which is invariably shewn by Govt. in similar instances more especially when the family of Kanchun Lal Late Moharir (Muhurrir) of the same thana received a pecuniary assistance for their maintenance a case in which the Maharir only pursued some Dacoits and on his return fell sick and died.

Your petitioner, etc.

Mossammat Seetal Daye alias Rajcoomari.

INDEX